"The book will be an eye-opener to patients and their families and should be required reading for anyone treating a person with an eating disorder. It will also emphasize to mental health providers and insurance companies that there are no shortcuts to treatment which often takes a very long time. Her description of the ingredients that make for effective treatment are a valuable contribution to the understanding of what contributes to recovery."

— **Alexander R. Lucas, M.D.**
Emeritus Professor of Psychiatry, Mayo Medical School
Emeritus Consultant, Section of Child and Adolescent
Psychiatry, Mayo Clinic

"*The Long Road Back* is a unique story, that of a recovered anorexic told by herself. It breaks new ground for anorexics everywhere."

— **Judith L. Rapoport, M.D.**
Child Psychiatry Branch, NIMH
Author, *The Boy Who Couldn't Stop Washing*

"Judy takes us to the heart of her pain and through the steps that led to recovery. Her inspiring story will give hope to families and individuals still in the bondage of an eating disorder. Judy's life is a witness that there is healing."

— **Gregory L. Jantz, Ph.D.**
Director, The Center for Counseling and Health
Resources, Inc.

"*The Long Road Back* is an openly frank exposure of one person's detailed and intimate look into the world of anorexia nervosa. The author's journey includes way stations of incompetent mental health professionals, the judicial system, hospitals, religion, and the ever-present movement from darkness to light. I highly recommend this book for anyone who wants to or needs to know what it is like for someone to have lived this devastating and painful life."

— **Terence J. Sandbek, Ph.D**
Author, *The Deadly Diet*

"Compelling, personal account of the '*The Long Road Back*' from the onset to recovery from anorexia nervosa. A very introspective look into the mind of an eating-disordered individual that reads like a well written novel. This book goes beyond the body image issues and looks into the emotional aspects with honesty and the ultimate uplifting movement toward recovery."
> — Ira M. Sacker, M.D.
>> Founder and Director of HEED—"Helping to End Eating Disorders"
>> Brookdale University Hospital and Medical Center
>> Author, *Dying to Be Thin*

"From the edge of the anorexic abyss, Judy has found the road to recovery. *The Long Road Back* so poignantly reveals the pain, struggle, deprivation, and betrayal she not only inflicted upon herself but endured at the hands of those whose job it was to help. Her book is a wonderful source of inspiration to sufferers and also a wake-up call to those providing care, that the treatment should not be worse than the disease itself. Recovery must be about respect, empowerment, and hope."
> — Gayle E. Brooks, Ph.D.
>> Clinical Director, Renfrew Center of Florida

"Judy Tam Sargent has written a sensitive and inspiring autobiography which proves that recovery from even severe anorexia is possible. This book will help anyone struggling with an eating disorder, as well as their caretakers and loved ones."
> —Lindsey Hall Cohn
>> Co-author, *Anorexia Nervosa: A Guide to Recovery*

"In a story that proves an eating disorder does not have to be for-ever or fatal, *The Long Road Back* is a wonderful gift of hope for recovery! Read it, and you will walk away awed by Judy's deter-mination, inspired by her encouraging words, and with a deeper understanding of what it takes to move beyond food and weight fears."

— **Cynthia Nappa Bitter**
Author, *Good Enough*...

"A young woman's harrowing journey through the hell of anorexia and an antiquated health-care system that had much to learn about what is needed for long-lasting and full recovery. BRAVO to this young woman's strength, determination, and courage to tell her truth and commitment to help others through the telling of her story. A strong testimonial to the human spirit's ability to heal despite the odds against it."

— **Jane E. Latimer, M.A.**
Author, *Beyond the Food Game* and *Eat with Love*

"Judy's graphic depiction of her unabated obsession with food and exercise, the agony of her chronic sleeplessness, bone-chilling cold and acute starvation, her hospitalizations, therapy and arduous path to recovery vividly reveal the thoughts and mind-set of a sufferer from anorexia. With poignant clarity, Judy describes the contribution to her road back of being treated with respect and humanity and encouraged to trust her own gut, as well as of her clinging to hope and taking steps toward owning responsibility for her life and happiness. I wish that I had learned much earlier in my life the life lessons Judy's struggle taught her."

— **Avis Rumney, M.A., M.A.**
Marriage and Family Therapist and Eating Disorder Specialist
Author, *Dying to Please: Anorexia Nervosa and Its Cure*

The Long Road Back

The Long Road Back
A Survivor's Guide to Anorexia

Judy Tam Sargent, R.N., M.S.N.

NORTH STAR
Publications
Georgetown, Massachusetts

Author's note: All of the names and places have been changed to protect the privacy of those involved.

For permissions and reprint information, contact North Star Publications:
P.O. Box 227
East Sandwich, MA 02537
Tel (978) 352-9976
Fax (978) 352-5586
email norbook@aol.com
www.ReadersNdex.com/northstar

Printed in Canada
Webcom Limited – Toronto

ISBN 0-880823-19-5

Edited by Sonia Nordenson
Cover design by Jeanne Marie White
Text design and composition by Jenna Dixon

Publisher's Cataloging-in-Publication
Sargent, Judy Tam
  The long road back : a survivor's guide to anorexia / Judy Tam
  Sargent. — 1st ed.
    p.   cm.
  Includes bibliographic references and index.
  ISBN: 0-880823-19-5
  1. Anorexia nervosa—Patients—United States—Biography.
  I. Title.
RC552.A5S37   1999
616.85/262/0092   QBI99-269

For all individuals currently suffering from anorexia nervosa and other eating disorders, with the hope that they, too, may find a full recovery

and

for my mother, without whose unending support and encouragement I wouldn't be here telling my story today.

Contents

Foreword

Anorexia nervosa is a tenacious and potentially fatal disease. It begins insidiously, often in a young woman who is bright, talented, and ambitious. Gradually it alters her carefree life, drawing her inward and isolating her from her family and friends. Inexplicably, her outward behavior changes, bewildering those who care about her. As she loses weight, progressively her body withers, her emotions constrict, and her mind becomes strained. There is no single cause, no typical childhood, and neither she nor her parents should be blamed for the illness. Many circumstances, including biological vulnerability, personality traits, and sociocultural influences work together to start the process. The disease takes hold, and eventually takes on a life of its own. It becomes all-consuming.

Finding appropriate treatment can be overwhelmingly difficult, even for the most sophisticated and knowledgeable families. Judy Tam Sargent has written a powerful and poignant narrative about her family's search for treatment and about the obstacles and pitfalls that stand in the way of recovery. She chronicles her struggles against anorexia nervosa through a dark nightmare of hospitals and diverse treatments. Her odyssey spanned many years and deprived her of an ordinary adolescence. With great frankness and remarkable insight, she describes the negative and positive aspects of the treatments she received.

As has been true for so many others, Ms. Sargent saw herself and her doctors as antagonists. But, unlike most, she remembers and articulates her experiences vividly. Some treatments were coercive, others used behavior modification aimed only to change outward behaviors, and still others used protocols that ignored her individuality. What many of the treatments had in common was that they were imposed without her consent and without considering her as a unique person. They were dehumanizing and humiliating. Consequently, she reacted with opposition and defiance. Nonetheless, as she caricatures her antagonists and describes the tricks that she and her fellow patients pulled off, one sees that her sense of humor was hardly extinguished. Yet, as the illness became her identity, she increasingly lost hope.

Healthcare providers must learn to understand that each patient is a unique individual. The treatment goals of the providers and those of the patient should be the same, and mutual trust and respect must develop before treatments can succeed. The patient must know that she is listened to, and must understand the importance of participating in her own treatment. Ms. Sargent confirms this by explaining that what made her well was her decision to become an active participant in the process. She also describes the qualities of those who were able to facilitate her ultimate recovery, as she gradually achieved personal mastery over her health and life. The persons and places she describes are real, but their names and locations are fictitious to protect confidentiality.

Judy Tam Sargent's experiences will help not only those afflicted with anorexia nervosa, but also their families. Her story can make health professionals aware of the thoughts and feelings of someone undergoing the illness, thus making the anorexic person somewhat easier to understand. A chapter of practical suggestions for those having the disorder, their families, and their therapists stems from experience, and is therefore particularly relevant.

This book can convey to insurance providers the realization that anorexia lasts a very long time and that superficial treatments only make it worse and prolong its course. Anorexia should be considered a catastrophic illness, and appropriate treatment provided for as long as necessary. If such support is provided, individualized, and continued with compassion, recovery from even the severest form of the condition does occur, and can lead to a productive and satisfying life.

— **Alexander R. Lucas, M.D.**
Emeritus Professor of Psychiatry, Mayo Medical School
Emeritus Consultant, Section of Child and Adolescent
Psychiatry, Mayo Clinic

Acknowledgments

I want to take this opportunity to thank George Trim, my publisher, for his incredible ability to see past the early rough edges of this book, and for his support and encouragement through the publishing process. Also, a special thank-you to my editors, Julie Ann Harrell and Sonia Nordenson, for their expert guidance, unending patience, and support through the editing process.

I would also like to thank all of the people who supported me through my illness and maintained their faith in my ability to recover, most especially Alexander R. Lucas, M.D., Victoria B. Buoen, M.D., and Noel R. Larson, Ph.D. Thank you, R.J.B., for always being there for me; your friendship is most highly treasured. A special thank-you to Karen Farchaus-Stein, Ph.D., for her academic and professional guidance and support. Finally, a thank-you to my family.

The following poem was written by my sister, Anne Catherine Sargent, who also contributed the poem on pages 143 and 144. My sister's poems provide a view of the anorexic experience from the perspective of a family member. I'm grateful that Anne has shared them with me for publication in this book.

Growing

I

Big sister, you used to walk with me
to Golden Hills Drugs for candy,
the streets of Minnesota holding us to this
earth. We didn't talk of mother loving you
as a mirror or of father in his nightly study,
we just followed each other through
shortcuts, dodging dogs, treading light
on ground we didn't own.

II

I was there when anorexia curved her
thin fingers toward you, beckoning. I was little
sister you put on the scale. Three years between us
you fed me steak-ums, weighing us,
one after the other. Your body bossing us
around. I didn't tell, not the counselor, not
mother with her busy eyes, not dad at his desk.
I watched you in the kitchen making me meals.

III

You shed yourself, old sister, gave it up,
handed it over, to anorexia, cult leader, sexless
lady. You joined the ranks in Mayo, in Madison,
you toured hospitals in your bones,
I went to see you but all I could see was the
gown, tube in your nose. Your glasses faced

the floor. Your foot jiggled at the end of your leg,
trying to go somewhere. If you wanted me,
you did not say.

IV

I was a teenager without you, sister of hospital smells,
of mother's emergency calls. How many times
were you *this close* to dead. I wished you
dead, I wished you alive, drinking soda, talking to
boys. I wished you my boyfriend, even. I was sixteen
and mad/states away, happy/you dying and
dying, your bones pulling at your skin.

V

Sister, alive, sister of anorexia, does she fight you,
does she talk to you at night? I don't know what to say
to you, you didn't say sorry, all of those years I waited
for you to make up your mind.

1

My Early Years

As a child, I learned that I couldn't believe in my own perceptions. Too often, the verbal and nonverbal messages I was given were incongruent.

Sometimes I would ask my mother why she was mad at me. In an angry voice, she would reply, "I'm not mad at you."

To that statement, I often countered, "Then why are you yelling at me?"

To this, she usually answered, "I'm not yelling at you!"

My instincts told me that my mother was mad at me. My ears told me that she was raising her voice. But my mother's spoken statements told me otherwise. Such situations made me feel crazy.

Today, I see the link between (1) my feelings of craziness and loss of control over my own life and (2) my need to place rigid restraints on my weight and eating. When other areas of my life felt out of control, there was always one thing I knew I *could* control. My weight and eating became the focus of my life, and all of my other troubles were forgotten—at least temporarily.

This book is my attempt to shed light on a deadly affliction. Few books currently available provide helpful suggestions from the standpoint of someone who has actually suffered (and recovered) from anorexia nervosa. The account that follows is not meant to be an attack on the mental health-care system, or on any one group of people. I'm writing my story in the hope that it will benefit young men and women currently suffering from anorexia, along with their therapists and family members.

The Beginnings of My Anorexia

I don't know when the illness actually began. My mother claims that she woke up one morning and I was anorexic. I believe it was a more gradual process, one that evolved over a period of time. After years of intensive therapy, I know that my early childhood experiences and consequent obsessive personality set the stage for anorexia nervosa.

To set the stage for my illness, I must first give you some family history.

On a cold, blustery January day in 1968, Bobby and I were born. We were the firstborn children. While she was carrying us, our mother got toxemia. When her physician couldn't reduce Mother's dangerously high blood pressure, he decided to perform an emergency cesarean section. Bobby and I were born shortly after nine in the evening, each weighing just over four pounds. After a year-long trial with a fertility drug, our parents were thrilled to have two healthy babies.

We had a happy early childhood. In my recollection, our family was the American dream come true. Mother was a nurturing, stay-at-home parent. I can remember walks in the park in our double stroller, and my family's notorious people stacks, when Bobby and I were posed at the top of a pyramid formation. I remember the fun of playing tag around the living room . . . afternoon naps in our crib, sharing toys and jabbering together . . . nights in my father's study, playing with trains.

I remember feeding Bobby ice cream sandwiches—one bite for me, then one for him. Maybe that should have been a clue that something wasn't right. Bobby didn't feed himself, talk as I did, or look at people. My parents didn't recognize the subtle signs. They were young, and we were their first children. Our early differences were easily passed off as personality traits.

Bobby and I had several playmates—two sets of twins, the children of my father's colleagues. It's not surprising that when my sister, Anne, was born in September of 1970, and my parents brought her home from the hospital, I asked, "Where's the other one?" My parents had to sit down with me and explain that all children didn't come in pairs.

Many years after I came to terms with Bobby's differences, I asked my mother, "When did you realize something was wrong?" Mother replied, "It was when your father brought you and Bobby to the hospital to visit me, right after I had Anne."

She told me that Bobby had stood at the foot of her bed, batting at his eyes with his hands and blinking madly, as if he had sand in his eyes. My mother had asked, "What's wrong with Bobby?"

From then on, Bobby's speech deteriorated and he displayed more of the classical autistic behavior. At home, my mother noticed that he looked at things only through his fingers, his hand over his face as a shield. Bobby began holding his hands in strange ways, always covering his eyes with one, the other rigidly fixed at his side. My brother, who had once run freely around the house, a Winnie the Pooh tucked under one arm, no longer engaged in ordinary play.

Bobby was very jealous of our new sister. He used to pull her hair. My parents remember the many times they had to pry Bobby's fingers out of Anne's tendrils. He used to knock over Anne's baby carrier, which led my mother to become concerned for Anne's safety. She hired someone to come to the house just to watch Bobby.

As time went on, Bobby stopped walking normally. My mother observed him walking backward through the house, his fingers covering his eyes, saying over and over again, "Woo woo woo." No amount of comfort or attention reduced the strange behaviors. My parents could no longer deny that something was terribly wrong with Bobby. The illusion of our perfect world was shattered, and I lost a part of my childish innocence.

My Brother's Autism

Bobby's diagnosis devastated our family. In an effort to find a cure for my brother's illness, my parents read all of the literature on his disorder. At that time, autism was not well understood. The medical profession theorized that autistic children were so emotionally traumatized by their cold and uncaring mothers that they retreated inward into a world of their own. One article suggested that the mother had to have subconsciously wished the child dead, leading to the autistic withdrawal.

The health-care profession now accepts autism as a developmental delay or a neurological disorder, not a childhood psychosis. There is mounting evidence for a structural abnormality in the brain that is associated with autism. Recent brain-autopsy studies of autistic people have shown structural neuronal or basic cellular stunting in the hippocampus and amygdala areas of the brain, areas that are responsible for information processing and emotion.

My parents, assuming that autism was a treatable psychiatric illness, wanted to find the best possible help for Bobby. They read extensively on the subject and called all of the major university medical centers. In their attempt to find an effective treatment option, they considered several large medical centers known for their work with autism. They finally chose the Cedarside Institute, a residential treatment center for emotionally disturbed children, located near Chicago.

The cost for residential treatment was astronomical and not covered by health insurance. As a professor of economics at the University of Minnesota, my father was just making ends meet. In anticipation of the bills for Bobby's residential care, which would consume nearly his entire annual salary, he took on a second job.

My brother and I were four when Bobby was sent away to the Cedarside Institute, in the spring of 1972. I vividly remember the day he left. We even have pictures: my mother's hair in curlers, Anne in green checkered overalls, smiling, not comprehending the situation, and me with a ponytail, dark circles under my eyes, innocence lost. All of my brother's toys lined our dining room floor, as if in anticipation of a burial ceremony. My parents packed the car with Bobby's toys, then loaded in my twin—my other half, my soulmate—and drove off in the morning sunlight. I watched from the kitchen window as the car rounded the corner into the calm spring day, carrying my best friend to some unknown fate. A part of my spirit died with Bobby's departure that morning, never to return.

After Bobby left, we entered a period of intense mourning, as if my brother had died. Sometimes I wonder if it would have been easier if Bobby *had* died, since our family could have grieved and moved on. As it was, we all seemed to get lost in the grieving process, no one speaking of the silent poison of sadness that oozed through our lives.

My parents were so sad that I knew better than to ask questions. They were already upset enough. My father never cried, yet now I saw him shed tears. We never ever talked about Bobby, because our family didn't talk about things. Within several months of Bobby's departure, I developed asthma.

I didn't see my twin again for six years. Since the medical profession believed that autism was a psychological response to parental abuse, my parents were allowed to visit him only once a year, for one hour, while being supervised in the visiting room. The Cedarside staff felt that any more visiting time would be psychologically harmful to Bobby. I can only imagine the guilt that my parents must have felt. My mother still cries today, and my father cannot talk about it.

When my parents sent Bobby to the Cedarside Institute, they told me that they were sending him to a special school so that he could get better and come home. Every year, when I blew out the candles on my birthday cake, I used to wish that my brother would get better and come home. It wasn't until my senior year in high school that I realized Bobby would never get better, would never come home.

Life After Bobby

After Bobby left, Anne and I grew closer. I remember many fun times with her, sneaking through backyards on our way to the candy store; dodging the neighbors' mammoth dog; hiding in the laundry chute, which we turned into our fort; and hanging from the limbs of a crab apple tree to practice our gymnastic skills. I recall carrying Heidi, the girl with muscular dystrophy, in our bright red wagon; playing with Froggy Bobby, our giant stuffed frog; and having tea parties with our favorite dolls.

Being about three years apart, we also displayed the typical sibling rivalry. We were either the best of friends or the worst of enemies. I, being older and more clever, often shuffled the blame onto Anne.

For example, one time my sister decided to play a prank on a teacher, and I offered to help. Anne had saved a motion sickness bag from an airplane, planning to toss it into her teacher's doorway with the words "barf bag" inscribed on it. This would have been innocent enough, but I decided that the bag would have more impact if it had something in it. I mixed a concoction of corn, ketchup, mustard, oatmeal, and anything gross I could find. Anne poured the mixture into the bag before tossing it into the teacher's office. When the teacher called my mother to tell her what had happened, my mother came to me and said, "You won't believe what Anne did today."

Anne was always getting in trouble, while I posed as the well-behaved one, so any blame was easily passed to her. I'm lucky that my sister still speaks to me today. For the most part, though, Anne and I were good friends.

As part of my privileged childhood, I was fortunate enough to have all kinds of lessons—everything from music to ballet to ice-skating. My mother served as a room mother for my classes at school. Anyone looking at our family from the outside would have thought we had it all.

The only thing about my grade-school years that I recall as difficult was our move from Minneapolis to Chicago and back again. My father took a one-year sabbatical to study at the University of Chicago, and spending my third-grade year in Chicago meant being close to my brother but being unable to see him.

My classroom overlooked Bobby's special school. He was so near, yet so far. I remember my mother taking me and Anne with her in the car, to follow a group from Bobby's school in an effort to catch a glimpse of him. I don't remember ever seeing him, just our attempts to spot him. We took many packages to my brother's school, since Mother baked goodies for Bobby every week: cheesecake, brownies, chocolate chip cookies—all of his favorites. When we were in Minneapolis, she mailed these packages, but while we lived in Chicago she hand-delivered them, hoping to catch sight of him.

Shortly before our return to Minneapolis, Anne and I were allowed to join my parents in their annual visit to Bobby. I remember the anticipation, remember walking into the eggshell-blue visiting room, passing the stately stairwell covered in oriental rugs and wondering if those were the same stairs that he would travel on his way into the room.

Tears welled in my eyes as I saw Bobby come round the corner. He was hardly recognizable—not the same little boy I had buried six years before. He was wearing overalls, with a red-and-blue striped shirt. I tried to talk to him. He replied by echoing my words as autistic children do. I felt alienated from him. What about our special language?

I sensed an incredible emptiness that day, a void, the cold hardwood floor beneath my feet seeming to accentuate the feeling. Now I better understood how my parents felt when they returned from each annual trip to see Bobby. I understood their sad faces, their silence, their unshed tears.

When we returned to Minneapolis, some of my old friends had moved and the others had formed cliques of which I was no longer a part. Going back to my old school, I felt left out and lonely. Not only had I lost my twin; I had now lost my peer connections. Depression began to cloud my days, and I started having nightmares. I remember wishing I were dead. I was ten years old.

In the years after Bobby left, my parents gradually grew apart. My father, trying to deal with the loss of his cherished son, isolated himself in his study. In the same way that an alcoholic soothes the pain by drinking, he dealt with Bobby's absence by burying himself in his work. My parents never fought, they just never spoke.

Once a week, my father took off several hours from work for a family outing. Sometimes he and I would play softball. He proudly told the Little League coach that I could throw the ball better than any boy my age. I hated softball, but I agreed to play because I knew how badly my father wanted a boy. Playing softball was the best thing I could do to try to make up for Bobby's loss.

Sometimes the whole family went cross-country skiing. My father, who has always been highly competitive, often raced off ahead of us, leaving my mother to bring up the rear with Anne. I usually wound up somewhere in the middle, trying to catch up with my father, for competition had been instilled in me from an early age.

The End of My Parents' Marriage

My parents' interactions dwindled to that one weekly outing. It's not surprising that my mother, still a homemaker rather than a career woman, grew lonely.

When I was ten, Brandon came into our lives. My father always had graduate students working for him. Sometimes, when the economics department was trying to lure someone from another school, my family would host the visitor as a houseguest for a brief time. Brandon was one of the precocious students that the department was trying to lure. A graduate student who had been working for my father, he came to live with us one summer.

I first met Brandon when I was visiting my father's office. Dad had told me, "I have someone for you to meet. He's really nice. He may come and live with us this summer." We all went to lunch. While eating a bowl of clam chowder, I scrutinized Brandon from across the table. He seemed nervous; his foot jiggled. After lunch, I told my father, "I don't know if I like him." Dad encouraged me to give him a chance.

I learned not to judge people on the first meeting, for Brandon was great fun. He was reserved in front of my parents, but the best of playmates when nobody was watching, giving me piggyback rides on the living-room floor. Brandon was like the father I had always wanted. I could talk to him and he didn't put me down. He became my friend and confidant.

The day Brandon came to live with us was the beginning of a long, harrowing three-year saga. I was not the only one who was drawn to Brandon's caring nature. My mother also responded to him. After years of loneliness in her own home, she found that Brandon offered her a sympathetic ear. He helped her with the dishes and paid attention to her. My mother fell in love. It was an emotional affair, not a physical one, yet it tore our family apart shred by shred.

Brandon stayed with us that first summer and returned to his primary home the following year. In his absence, my mother's feelings didn't dissipate. She became more aware of the void that had developed in her relationship with my father after the loss of a child and so many years of silence. On some nights I was awakened by asthma. Venturing to the kitchen to get my medication, I'd find my mother curled in a corner of the dining room, sitting on the hardwood floor and softly weeping as if to release years of unspoken sadness. At ten, I knew that my parents' marriage would not last.

My mother, too, must have anticipated the divorce. She found a job as a statistical computer programmer at the Federal Reserve Bank of Minneapolis, one of the two places where my father worked. The rift between my parents continued to grow. For three years, Brandon returned each summer to help my father with his research.

When I was twelve, my parents separated on the eve of my father's birthday. I clearly recall the night. Anne and I were going to "camp out" in a tent set up in her bedroom. I had just finished baking a chocolate cake for the coming day. Anne and I played board games till it was past midnight, then fell asleep. At two o'clock, I awoke to hear doors slamming. What was wrong? My parents never slammed doors. Was dad kicking Brandon out of the house? *I'd better stay in my room*, I thought. My heart pounding, I fell back to sleep.

At five o'clock, a strange silence filled the house. My eyes popped open; something was wrong. I woke Anne and we crept around the house, to find that it was empty. We were the only ones there. My father, my mother, and Brandon were all gone. We cried, and waited, and cried some more. I tried to comfort Anne when she asked, "Are Mom and Dad getting divorced?" "No, of course not," I replied.

Nobody returned until eleven o'clock that night. My mother arrived first, and told us what had happened. She and Dad were getting a divorce because my father had asked for one. He didn't come home that night. I sliced the birthday cake that I had so lovingly made and fed it, piece by piece, to the garbage disposal, my stubborn illusion of the perfect family finally washing down the drain. Maybe it was then that my aversion to food began. Perhaps it was that night in 1980 that food became a symbol of hopes and dreams lost forever.

Taking Sides

During the separation, my father was severely depressed. I was worried about him. (Dad's brother had committed suicide when *his* marriage ended.) For the first several weeks, I went to stay with my father, camped out in a sleeping bag on the living-room floor of his new apartment. Then I became homesick for the house I had grown up in, for my mother and sister, for the neighborhood with my childhood friends. Like most children of divided parents, I felt emotionally torn.

I desperately wanted approval and acceptance from each of my parents. I loved them both, equally. But, during the separation and divorce, I constantly felt that I had to take sides with one or the other. I was forced to decide which parent I wanted to live with. It was a horrible feeling because, either way, one parent was going to be disappointed. The people-pleaser part of me could not win. I ended up choosing my mother.

My mother worked in the same department as my father, and naturally a lot of rumors were flying around. People in the office were speculating that my mother and Brandon were having an affair. So Mom sent me in to put a stop to the rumors. At the time, not even I knew what was true, but I went in to set things straight for her anyway. I walked into the offices of my father's colleagues and said, "I don't know what you've heard, but I want to assure you that none of it is true." I felt like a liar, telling people these things when I didn't myself know the truth. In retrospect, I realize that it was unfair to send a twelve-year-old on such an errand.

My parents took turns watching over Anne and me when there was no school. Often we had to go to work with them. My father used to pacify us with candy. We would read and eat taffy. Sometimes we interrupted Brandon's work to get him to play a practical joke with us. One time, Brandon helped us fill another graduate student's drawer with cornflakes. We supplied the idea and Brandon supplied the cornflakes. We made a good team.

It's likely that my lack of control over my own life set the stage for my future eating disorder. When I went to my parents' workplace, people treated me differently according to which parent I was with at the time. If I was with my father, they treated me well. If I was with my mother, they snubbed me and treated me as if I were the one who'd had the affair. Given my lack of healthy boundaries, I then felt guilty for Mom.

No More "Perfect" Parents

After the divorce, my mother's relationship with Brandon quickly faded. When Brandon disappeared from my mother's life, he also disappeared from mine. This was the man that I had grown to care about: my second father, my confidant and friend, the one who listened to my worries and fears. I was confused. If my mother and father no longer got along with Brandon, did that mean that I could no longer be friends with him? The answer was an unequivocal yes. My father became irate if I even tried to discuss the issue. It was a closed matter, so once again I had to push my feelings of loss and sadness from my mind. My loneliness grew, for I had lost yet another friend.

My mother fell into a series of chaotic relationships. Anne and I nicknamed the man she dated after Brandon "Veggie." He was a vegetarian, and not fond of kids.

Late one evening, Anne came to me and said, "Let's put peanut butter in the tips of his shoes."

"No," I told her. "We'd better not do that. When he puts on his shoes to go home, we're going to get in trouble. We have to be more subtle." I shared my improved plan: "We ought to cover his car with peanut butter."

With an economy-sized jar of peanut butter in hand, Anne and I stole out into the night. I used a sponge, while Anne smeared the lumpy stuff directly with her bare hands. All of a sudden, some downstairs lights came on. Veggie was getting ready to leave. Without warning Anne of the danger that loomed, I ran around the house and entered through the back door.

Anne got caught. My mother came to me and said, "Look what your sister has just done!" I replied empathetically, "I can't believe it. That's *terrible*. Can I help clean it up?"

There were other unsuitable men, like John, who was seventeen years younger than my mother—not much older than me. Nevertheless, John tried to act like my father. I felt as if I needed to protect my mother from these men. Sometimes it was as if I were the parent and she the child. I often felt aged beyond my years.

Mother's behavior during those years destroyed my belief that my parents were perfect. I'd had a conservative upbringing, and had internalized the strong moral values with which I was raised.

Those values included not having an affair while married and not sleeping with anyone you weren't married to. Now I was learning that there were two sets of standards: those that applied to my mother and those that applied to me.

In addition to the family factors that contributed to my illness, my innate personality helped to fuel the anorexic process. I've always been a perfectionist and a people pleaser. As a child, I wanted to get perfect grades in school. I strove to be the best and to make my parents and teachers happy. I cried if I got the second highest grade on a test. When other kids used to go out and play at recess, I stayed in and compulsively worked on advance homework assignments. I was well liked by my teachers, and I rarely got into trouble.

My perfectionism had its good side. It allowed for my rapid progress in school and in other areas of my life. However, when it came to my compulsive pursuit of thinness, these seemingly harmless perfectionistic traits would lead me down a dangerous road and provide major obstacles to my recovery. Throughout my childhood, the groundwork was well laid for my future descent into anorexia nervosa.

2

Adolescence, Asthma, and Anorexia

After my parents' separation, my asthma flared up. I was hospitalized numerous times when the attacks were severe. My allergist suggested that I see a psychologist to help decrease my stress level and thereby get my asthma under control.

The psychologist, Dr. Phillip Brown, was a tall man with a warm smile and chocolate-colored skin. I was desperate for someone to talk to about my family situation, so I welcomed seeing Dr. Brown. I saw him once a week for about a year. During our sessions, I spilled my guts to him in hopes that he could help me counteract my feelings of helplessness about my family situation.

I wish I could say that the sessions helped me, but they didn't. The only thing I remember is that I repeatedly told Dr. Brown how helpless I felt. His reply was always a variation on the same theme: "Well, that's the way it is, so you just have to get used to it." I left the sessions feeling even more helpless than I had felt initially.

Dr. Brown's favorite statement served only as a confirmation that my life was beyond my own control. Toward the end of our sessions, as part of a self-devised self-improvement campaign, I began losing weight. This proved to be the beginning of my long bout with anorexia nervosa. Of course, Dr. Brown couldn't know this. He ended our sessions by pronouncing me cured, despite my mother's concerns about my weight loss.

A Fear of Being Fat

Most young girls go through a period of weight gain around the time of puberty, and I followed this norm. When it came to junk food, I was a typical teenager. I was also a competitive swimmer, which gave me a ravenous appetite.

It wasn't an easy time for me. My father used to weigh me, and he'd make comments about my increasing weight. I remember one time when Dad had just prepared supper. He set a plate of spaghetti on the table in front of me and then asked, "So, Judy, how's your weight going?" My father didn't want to know what I thought about my weight. It was just his subtle way of saying, "You look fat. You shouldn't eat so much." I sat through the whole supper without eating a bite, then went to my room and cried.

I was a straight-A student, I was third-chair first violin in the school orchestra, and I had taken third place in my event in the State Finals swim competition. However, I was fat. I vowed then and there that I would change that. In an attempt to protect myself from further criticism, I declared that I would no longer stay at my father's house for any length of time. This only widened the rift between Dad and me. First I had chosen to live with my mother. Now I refused to spend time with him. I was no longer Dad's perfect little girl.

From the time I was young, my parents were noticeably concerned with their own weight. They were both avid runners, and prone to fad diets. I remember my mother, weighing all of one hundred and four pounds at a height of five feet two inches, telling me how fat she was. I'm sure that my parents' preoccupation with thinness influenced my own weight obsession.

I was never really fat. Perhaps I ate more than I needed to, but I certainly wasn't fat. Prior to my weight loss, I reached an all-time high of one hundred fourteen pounds. I am five feet three inches tall. I was taking Prednisone for my asthma, which gave me the moon face characteristic of those who take that drug, along with the associated weight-distribution changes. Some of the kids at school called me "Chipmunk Cheeks." Their teasing only added to the shakiness of my self-esteem.

In an effort to feel better about myself, I embarked on a weight-loss campaign when I was about thirteen. It started with a simple diet. I didn't know much about dieting. I began by eating only low-calorie foods. I didn't lose much weight because I hadn't yet figured out that I had to cut down the portion sizes. I ate huge bowls of vegetable soup and spaghetti sauce, just the sauce, after swim-team practice. In addition, I started to make rules for myself about what I could and could not eat. My eating patterns gradually became bizarre.

Unsuccessful Bulimia

One day, I decided to try making myself throw up. I must have gotten the idea from reading an article about bulimia. I went downstairs and locked myself in the bathroom, leaned over the toilet bowl, and stuck my fingers down my throat, just as the article had described. I gagged and gagged, my face turning red and purple and every color in between, but I was unable to make myself vomit. The article was wrong. They had lied. There must have been some secret that they failed to share. I thought to myself, "I'm not trying this again. This is miserable." From upstairs, I heard my mother calling, "Judy, where are you?" I washed my face with cold water, recomposed myself, and went back upstairs, hoping my mother wouldn't notice my bloodshot eyes.

A Formula for Dieting Success

When I was fifteen, I reached the awkward stage that most teenage girls go through. My breasts were developing, and my mother wanted to take me shopping for some new bras. We went to the local Sears store, where my mother picked out some full-figure bras for me to try on, commenting, "You're much more shapely than I was at your age." I decided then and there that I must eliminate the fullness of my breasts, for they were a symbol of my growing femininity and responsibilities.

After two years of unsuccessful dieting, I came upon a formula for success. I started the weight loss by simply cutting back on what I ate. I began by cutting back on portion sizes, then eliminated certain foods from my diet. When the weight loss didn't occur as quickly as I would have liked, I added exercise into the formula. The weight loss happened gradually. I went from one hundred four-teen pounds down to one hundred ten pounds. I noticed that I started to feel better. Then I set a new goal for myself, thinking, *I'd be happier if I weighed one hundred and five pounds.* When I got down to one hundred five, I thought, *This is great. If I feel this good now, just think how much better I'd feel at one hundred pounds.*

As my weight fell, I noticed that it was becoming difficult to lose any more pounds. So I restricted my food intake even further, eliminating pastas, most starches, all meats, and any liquids con-taining calories, until all I was allowing myself to eat was vegetables. I started reading calorie books avidly, and stopped eating breakfast. As the illness progressed, I began refusing to eat lunches at school and dinners at home with my family, saying "I already ate" or "I'm really not hungry" or "I'll eat later"—anything to get others off my back. My weight continued to fall.

I developed strange rituals around food, eating only secretly at night, after everyone had gone to sleep. I ate foods in the tiniest amounts, cut them into a zillion pieces, arranged them in special patterns on my plate, and chewed them until they could no longer be chewed. I relished my self-restraint, a testimony to my will power. This time, I was winning at the weight-loss game.

Out of Control

Yet something was seriously wrong. The weight loss had taken on a power and a life all its own. I was down to ninety-two pounds and still not happy, so I felt compelled to lose more weight. During lunch periods, I stole out behind the school yard to run on the track, in a frantic attempt to burn calories and lose more ugly pounds. After school and before my mother came home from work, I jogged the streets of Minneapolis, pounding the pavement, running until my feet bled, symbolically running away from my worries in an unconscious effort to disappear.

I became afraid to swallow my food. In response to this new fear, I came up with a solution. I began to chew my food and then spit it out into a napkin. I hid a plastic bag in my closet for just that purpose. Sometimes I thought, *Normal people don't do this. What's wrong with me? I can't possibly tell anybody what's going on. They'll think I'm crazy.* I felt horribly guilty. The shame was overwhelming.

I became afraid to drink anything, including water. I waited all day to take a drink, my mouth dry as a desert, my body crying out in agony. If I was terribly thirsty, I could divert my attention from my extreme hunger by thinking about where and when I would drink my next glass of water.

I also weighed myself many times each day. I weighed myself before drinking something and after, with clothes and without, in a crazy ritual gone awry. When my mother confiscated the bathroom scale, I walked three miles to the local YMCA to use their scale. Anorexia nervosa had completely taken hold of me. I was now a slave to it. My actions were no longer governed by rational thought, but by an insane desire for the ultimate thinness.

As an alcoholic conceals his drink, I always wore huge, bulky sweaters so my increasing thinness wouldn't be obvious to others. I didn't want anyone to try to stop me. But eventually there was no denying the fact that something was wrong.

My mother later told me, "I knew something was wrong the Thanksgiving that I watched you eat at the Hendersons' house. You hardly ate. You pushed your food around your plate, and it made everyone at the table really uncomfortable."

Losing weight had been a relatively quick and easy process. Unfortunately, freeing myself from the powerful grip of anorexia would be neither quick nor easy. The illness would eventually take over my entire being, leaving me only a shadow of the young woman I used to be. As my sense of identity diminished along with my body, anorexia would dominate me to the point where I "became the illness."

Locked Up

My first hospitalization for anorexia nervosa came on the eve of my sixteenth birthday. Needless to say, this was no sweet-sixteen party for me. I was young, and knew nothing of the workings of the mental-health system. I wish I could have stayed that way—young and naive. But I quickly began to adapt to the harsh reality of life in a hospital environment.

I entered Memorial Hospital fully intending to do my very best to cooperate and get better. Because of my struggles as an outpatient, my admission to the hospital actually came as a relief. Finally someone would help me get my life back under control! Or so I thought.

I still remember my first moments on Station Two North, the Adolescent Crisis Unit. I walked through a pair of heavy metal doors that slammed shut and locked behind me. The full implications of those doors didn't strike me until later. Locked doors eventually took on great significance for me, for they represented my loss of freedom. People who commit terrible crimes are locked up in prisons. During this hospital stay (and many future ones), I would sometimes ask, "What crime did I commit? What have I done that I have to be locked up?" The staff members always evaded these questions. They probably thought me somewhat paranoid, and documented my questions as evidence of that.

Past the doors, I walked down a long, stark hallway, with barren walls and furniture that looked made to weather the centuries. A few young people stood around outside their rooms, not doing much of anything because there was nothing for them to do. Kids didn't go to school on the short-term crisis unit. A boom box was blaring in the background.

As we rounded the corner, two boys in their early teens were standing near the nurses' station, arguing with a male staff member and spouting obscenities. One of the boys was saying, "That's not fair. It (expletive) says in my program that I can use the phone. I (expletive) hate it here."

As I toured the new surroundings, I thought, *What have I gotten myself into?* I'd been raised to have a low tolerance for vulgar language. Would I be able to make it here? Many ideas crossed my mind: *Maybe this is a mistake. I can probably just snap out of it on my own and start eating, if I just put my mind to it. I really don't belong here.*

We walked past a blue-padded seclusion room and arrived at the next door on the hallway, right by the nurses' station. Sabrina, the nurse, announced, "This is your room." Then, she turned to my mother and said, "We put her right by the nurses' station so we can keep a close eye on her." I asked myself, *Why do they have to keep a close eye on me? Don't they trust me?*

After my mother left, I saw that several kids were staring at me from across the hallway. They had a direct-line view into my room. They didn't look friendly, and their street-smart language offended me. I later learned that most of the others on this unit had conduct disorders or adjustment disorders. I was always considered a brain in school—prim, proper, and well behaved. Our differing styles didn't mix well. I kept to myself, and my loneliness and isolation grew.

The staff members kept to themselves as well. They spent most of their time behind the glass-enclosed nurse's station and only a small portion of time on the unit with us. I felt like I lived in a fish bowl. A thin wall of glass separated us from the staff, a barely visible line dividing the two realities. I often wondered if they were afraid of us. Why did they seclude themselves behind the glass wall? Was it a form of invisible protection?

Allison

I chose to associate with only two people on Station Two North. One of them was Allison, who walked up and greeted me right after I arrived on the unit. It was hard not to stare at her. She looked as if she had come directly from a concentration camp, her legs tiny sticks that jutted out from under an oversized shirt, her wispy blonde hair framing deep blue eyes that seemed much too large for her bony face. Allison was a young anorexic patient who knew the ropes. This was not her first hospitalization. Despite her youth, she was what I would call a seasoned anorexic.

At eleven, Allison had already learned how to play the game. I watched her thin frame dart up and down the hallways. There was lots of energy in her step, a bright smile on her face. She was helping the staff members by carrying items back and forth, in what I recognized as a secret attempt to burn calories. I watched Allison in the dining room, smiling as she spoke to the staff member at our table and covertly loading her napkin with items from her plate, to be discarded later in the nearby trash receptacle. I thought, *She couldn't possibly have the same problem I have. She looks way too happy and has far more energy than I do.* I had a lot to learn from Allison.

Stacy

One afternoon, I heard that we were getting a new patient. Allison always knew what was going on, so I went to find her.

"We're getting another eating-disordered person," Allison told me.

Feeling my competitiveness flare within me, I asked, "Is she anorexic?"

"No, I don't think so," Allison said. "I overheard a staff member saying that she's bulimic."

I was relieved to learn that the new patient would not be competing for the coveted position of skinniest anorexic.

Stacy arrived in the mid-afternoon, and was escorted to a room at the end of the hallway. I was envious of her from the outset. Why did she get to have a room at the end of the hall when I was placed directly in front of the nurses' station? Stacy was one year older than me, or seventeen. She was of normal weight, with sandy brown hair and a bad case of acne. By observing her, I verified right away that she was bulimic.

Even though I hadn't been vomiting, my bathroom was kept locked, but for some reason Stacy's bathroom was unlocked. Stacy used to sneak around the unit, steal food and eat it, and then vomit in her bathroom. It was no secret; she almost boasted about it. She went into all the gory details, telling me how she made herself vomit—as if I cared. Stacy had no self-control. I felt superior to her because I didn't vomit and I was skinny.

Stacy was always trying to talk to me. One of her first remarks to me was that we were just alike. I remember thinking, *No, we're not alike. You gross me out. I don't stick my finger down my throat and vomit like you.* Despite my negative feelings about Stacy, I quickly learned that if I were to survive on Station Two North, I would need someone to talk to. Allison and Stacy would have to do.

More Doctors

Prior to my admission, I'd started seeing Dr. Julia Holland, a clinical psychologist. Dr. Holland was a heavy woman with graying hair and oversized glasses. During our therapy sessions, I often became distracted by the sight of her wiggling flesh as she moved her arms about, gesturing vigorously with her hands. *God forbid that I ever let myself look like that,* I thought.

My pediatrician had referred me to Dr. Holland, and I wondered why he had sent me to someone who obviously had a weight problem in the other direction. Just looking at Julia Holland scared me, so it's not surprising that I couldn't talk to her as easily as I could talk to Dr. Brown. Besides, I had decided that talking would never solve my problems, never bring back my brother, and never put our family back together again. Yet I agreed to see Dr. Holland, to pacify my family and—later—to gain my freedom from the psychiatric ward. I continued therapy with her throughout my hospital stay, and for two further years.

In addition to Dr. Holland, I now had Dr. Bernard Lange, the psychiatrist in charge of my care at Memorial Hospital. Dr. Lange was an older man with dark hair and a thick, bushy beard. He stopped by my room several times a week, and always carried my chart with him. One morning, standing in my barren room, he said, "I see that your weight is down. You weigh eighty-two pounds today. That means we'll be taking away your books, and of course you'll have to stay in your room. You're allowed to come out of your room only for meals. No visitors or telephone, either."

During my hospitalization, I thought of Dr. Lange as "the weight man." While I was on Station Two North, he kept me on a strict behavior-modification program. My privileges, or lack thereof, were contingent upon my weight. According to the behavior-modification plan, privileges included everything from an unlocked bathroom to visits from my family, use of the telephone, access to my school books, the freedom to leave my room or wear my own clothes, and passes away from the unit. Dr. Lange was the person who controlled these privileges.

Getting Nowhere Fast

Life at Memorial Hospital wasn't easy for me, as was made evident by my consequent lack of privileges. I'd entered Station Two North with the hope that people would be supportive, that someone would help me, that I'd make good progress. I found just the opposite to be true.

Sabrina, the nurse who had admitted me to the unit, became my primary caregiver. She was a young woman of short stature, with long, curly brown hair and tortoiseshell glasses. Sabrina and I didn't get along from the very start. During my admission session, she asked me, "Why don't you just eat? Around here, you need to do what we say." I remember wondering, *What makes her think I'm not going to do what they say? Why is she already angry with me when I haven't done anything?*

My first meals on the unit were hard for me. I would sit at the table, my anxiety building, with a pounding heart and a lump in my throat. I was on a weight-gain meal plan of three thousand calories a day. When my tray came up on the metal cart, it was covered with fattening foods. I wanted to escape, but the locked door served as a constant reminder that there was only one way out.

I had dreamed of a supportive staff member who would talk to me when I cried and ease my fears. Well, that was fantasy and this was reality. A staff member glanced over our trays after we had eaten, but that was the extent of the mealtime supervision.

I would stare down at my breakfast tray, which held grape juice, a carton of whole milk, a large bowl of cereal, a sticky-sweet Danish roll, two slices of toast smeared with butter, and scrambled eggs drenched in grease. I wanted to die; I wanted to cry; I wanted to get up from the table and go running from the unit. I couldn't eat—not today. Maybe tomorrow. *How do they expect me to go from eating no breakfast to eating this?* I wondered. Then I'd slide the tray back into its slot on the metal cart and leave the dining room.

A Prison Within a Prison

Before long, I was confined to my room because of failure to gain weight. I told the staff I wasn't going to stay in my room, because I hadn't done anything wrong. In rebellion, I took to the hallways. That was a foolish move, for I was then locked in my room. It was at that point that I decided to wage my own quiet war against the staff. Initially, I had access to my schoolbooks, so I spent my days reading and exercising. Prior to my admission, I had become obsessed with running, so I found it comforting to jog in the corner of my room. Eventually, all of my books, clothing, and possessions were taken away. I was clothed in a hospital gown. All that I had in my room was a stark white mattress, which lay on the floor, and myself. I was allowed to leave my room only to attend meals. I wasn't allowed to have any visitors.

Depression began to sweep over me. I spent hours in my sterile white room, crying years of unspilled tears, a perpetual black cloud over my head. Given the same situation, anyone would have been depressed. My life was falling apart; I quite literally had nothing. Physically, I was starving. Emotionally, I was lonely and depressed. I had never been more isolated or alone. Looking back now, I wonder if any of the psychologists, psychiatrists, or staff members ever tried imagining themselves in the same situation, or thought of how it might feel. I doubt it.

I stayed in that room for a month. I spent my days trying to sleep away the boredom and depression, or exercising in the corner of my room. Every time I awoke from my fitful bouts of sleep, I awoke to the harsh reality of Station Two North. Exercise, sleep, and eating (or not eating) became the only variables over which I had control. I was determined not to give up this last little bit of control I had over my life, for I felt that if I did, I would cease to be.

Playing the Game

Before being confined to my room, I'd been amazed at how well Allison got by. The staff on the unit considered her a model patient. Eventually, I too learned the ropes. I realized that, in order to get through my stay on Station Two North, I needed to be able to play the game. This meant two things: doing what they wanted me to do and increasing my weight. When I saw them at meals, Allison and Stacy taught me all of their tricks. These included ways to hide food during mealtimes, methods for artificially inflating my weight, and vomiting. In the month that I was on Station Two North, I learned to play the game quite well. In fact, too well.

What nobody seemed to understand was that my weight was not the problem. Gaining twenty, thirty, or even forty pounds wouldn't make me well. Prior to my admission, my life and my self-esteem had revolved around my weight. I had weighed myself numerous times each day. And now the staff's focus on my weight was only making this obsession worse.

I knew that the staff wanted me to gain weight, so I gained weight for them. But it was artificial weight. As soon as I caught on to what I needed to do, I spent a week playing the hospital's game by drinking progressively greater amounts of water before my morning weigh-ins. I had an alarm clock, and I knew when they'd be coming to weigh me. Two eight-ounce cups of water weigh a pound; it's a matter of simple mathematics. Near the end of my stay, I was drinking as much as twenty cups of water each morning.

To keep me from drinking water before the morning weigh-in, the staff locked my bathroom every night. But I found a way around this. I secretly collected Styrofoam cups and filled them each evening before bedtime, hiding them under my bed. Several days in a row, I drank so much water that I vomited and had to start all over again.

My weight gain pleased the staff, and that was what mattered. Nobody thought to question the fact that I was gaining weight despite my continued refusal to eat. I was discharged from the hospital.

When I was released, the staff recommended to my parents that I be placed in long-term residential treatment. Tearfully, I told my mother, "You can't send me to long-term treatment. Please, Mom, you can't. I'm serious—if you send me there I'll kill myself!" I couldn't imagine spending another month the same way I'd just spent the previous one. My mother took me home.

It's a shame that my time on Station Two North wasn't put to better use. My first hospitalization was an important experience that would indirectly influence all my later hospital stays. Unfortunately, the experience was a negative one. Before my sojourn at Memorial Hospital, I was young, impressionable, and still naive about the workings of the mental-health-care system. I entered my first hospitalization with no preconceived notions. I had a sincere desire to get better, as well as a trusting attitude toward mental-health professionals.

During my stay on Station Two North, all that changed. I left Memorial Hospital completely disillusioned with the mental-health-care system. The staff's attempts to control me with a strict behavior-modification program had only caused me to cling to anorexia all the more fervently. My eating disorder took on new significance, for I now realized that eating (or not eating), exercise, and my obsessive-compulsive rituals were the last things in my life over which I had control. To make matters worse, I had learned that I was quite alone in my predicament.

3

Released But Not Cured

I returned home to Minneapolis and my family and friends. As I embarked upon my last two years of high school, memories of Memorial Hospital still haunted me, yet my life resumed a semblance of normalcy. In school, I continued to excel academically. I joined the cheerleading squad and once again became a school orchestra member.

I'd been set free from that horrible place called Station Two North, but I was still anorexic—in fact, more so than ever.

The Game Goes On

Every week, my mother scheduled me for a therapy session with Dr. Holland. I used to drive myself (I had my own car now) to our meetings in a historic neighborhood of Minneapolis. I found these sessions to be a boring waste of time. Maybe I never gave Dr. Holland a chance, for I had acquired a basic distrust of mental-health-care professionals and she was one of them. Also, Dr. Holland was such a large lady herself that I wasn't impressed when she told me I didn't have to worry about being fat. She was a fine one to talk, I thought. I didn't want to look like her!

Dr. Holland also had a hot temper. During one of my family therapy sessions, Anne, who was sitting on the end of the couch pulling a piece of taffy into a long string, remarked, "I'm just wondering if you're competent to treat my sister. No offense intended, but you don't seem to know what you're doing." Dr. Holland lost all her professional composure. She stood up and started yelling so loudly that I was afraid she might hit my sister. At that point, I lost whatever respect I'd had for her. After that, I often canceled my appointments with Dr. Holland—without my mother's knowledge, of course. I came up with some pretty creative excuses.

After my discharge from Station Two North, I was supposed to be weighed once or twice a week by Dr. Sheila Olson, a pediatrician. I went to these scheduled appointments for only a short while. I'd sit in a waiting room full of screaming babies and read old issues of *Parent Magazine*, waiting to be ushered by some nurse to the scale. I quickly learned the futility of these visits and quit going. As far as I could tell, Dr. Olson was just like the rest of the health-care professionals I'd met: not too bright. On my way to her office, I used to make a regular stop in the bathroom, where I'd fill up with as much water as I could drink without vomiting. Then I'd assemble my ankle weights, making sure I secured them well around my chest. Dr. Olson never suspected a thing.

Thus, my appointments with Dr. Holland and Dr. Olson were a complete waste of money and valuable time. My interactions with them only reconfirmed that I was in my predicament alone. I had escaped the locked doors of Station Two North, but was still my own prisoner. Those doors on Station Two North had keys to open them, but no one seemed to have the key to unlock my prison of anorexia.

A Secret Certainty

The two years following my hospitalization at Memorial Hospital weren't easy ones for me. My eating disorder was worse than ever, and I was even more alone. My waking moments were filled with obsessive thoughts and the need to perform rituals in order to keep myself feeling safe. These obsessions and rituals had been with me before, but they became much worse after my stay on Station Two North.

I'd never heard of anyone who was similarly afflicted, and I was convinced that I was completely crazy. This became my biggest secret. I believed that I had some horrible psychiatric affliction that nobody had ever heard of, and that I needed to conceal this awful secret from everyone. Only much later did I learn that many anorexics suffer from obsessive-compulsive tendencies, and that I wasn't crazy.

The Art of Vomiting

During this time, I added a new eating-disorder behavior to my repertoire: bulimia. I finally mastered the art of vomiting. At first it was difficult. Even though I'd been coached by Allison and Stacy, it took me hours of effort to achieve the goal. But before long, I could vomit at the drop of a hat.

Do you remember how I accidentally made myself puke when I was trying to inflate my weight with large amounts of water? Well, that experience proved to be the secret to my success. At first, I used vomiting just for those emergency occasions when I was forced to eat in front of others. On those occasions, the upchucking (when resorted to a little later) provided an easy out. Eventually, I had to vomit whenever I ate *any*thing. I felt compelled to get rid of anything and everything in my stomach.

After years of starvation, my body cried out so urgently for food that I gave in . . . and started a cycle of bingeing. I ate and ate until I couldn't eat any more, until my stomach hurt. I ate entire boxes of cookies, loaves of bread, a half-gallon of ice cream—anything I could get my hands on. Then the anxiety set in. I remember thinking, *What have I just done? I have absolutely no will power.* That was when I had to vomit.

I started out vomiting in normal places like the bathroom. But as my illness progressed and I felt a growing need to conceal the truth, I sometimes had to find alternative places such as plastic bags. Often I used the bathtub drain, where I could hide the sound of my vomiting by running the water. My family became a frequent customer of Roto-Rooter, and my weight loss continued.

I was still getting nearly perfect grades in school, but malnutrition was taking its toll on my thought processes. My thinking slowed dramatically. As a further hindrance, I was preoccupied by my obsessive thoughts. In order to maintain the good grades I had once attained so easily, I was forced to study much harder and for greater lengths of time. The amount of energy that anorexia and bulimia drain out of one is incredible. I was just plain exhausted all of the time.

A Promise

During my senior year in high school, my calculus teacher requested a parent-teacher conference with my mother. Mr. Flanagan was my favorite math teacher. He had taught my Analysis course the previous year, and he was like a grandpa to me. He never talked to me about the anorexia, but I'm sure that everyone who saw me knew that I had it.

Mr. Flanagan told my mother that he knew I was anorexic and implored her to do something about it. He suggested an inpatient treatment program in Wisconsin, designed specifically for adolescents with eating disorders. He knew someone who had been through the program and had supposedly recovered. When Mom got home, she called the doctor that Mr. Flanagan had recommended and made an appointment.

On a cold day in early November, my mother and I started out for Milwaukee to meet Dr. Bailey. We were driving, but as we progressed a severe snowstorm overtook us. We were forced to complete the last leg of our travel by Greyhound bus, arriving several hours late for my appointment. From the bus station, Mom and I took a taxi to the annex, a little building adjoining the main hospital.

I was quickly ushered into an exam room, where I waited in nervous anticipation. I heard a knock on the door, then the doctor entered. Dr. Bailey was a short man with dark hair, a mustache, and a stern face. He held out his hand, saying, "Hi. It's nice to meet you. I'm Dr. Bailey." *I'd better not try playing games with this guy*, I thought. *He looks serious.*

Dr. Bailey and my mother soon determined that I should be admitted to the inpatient unit at Presbyterian Hospital without delay. I wasn't happy about entering another hospital. This was my senior year in high school, and I didn't want to miss class time. Also, I'd learned from my previous admission that I couldn't trust mental-health professionals. However, it looked as if my stay on Three South (the inpatient eating disorders unit) would be different from my previous hospitalization.

My new doctor was a pediatric endocrinologist—someone who deals with childhood diabetes and other disorders of the endocrine system—not a psychiatrist. I'll never forget the promise Dr. Bailey made to me during that first meeting. He told me, in no uncertain terms, "I will make you better."

I wish that Dr. Bailey's promised healing could have materialized. In any event, that promise would be the foundation of my renewed hope for months to come.

4

The Adolescent Eating Disorders Unit

My mother and I took an elevator to the third floor, where we stepped out into a cold, white, heavily traveled hallway. We rounded a corner and went through some big doors to arrive at the nurses' station. My first impressions were encouraging. I walked onto Three South expecting locked doors and found the unit open—anyone could come and go as they pleased. I peered through a glass window into the main dayroom and saw the nurses clustered there, interacting with the patients.

As Mom and I toured the unit, we entered a green dayroom with floor-to-ceiling windows overlooking the street. A college-age girl with short blonde hair and a warm smile walked up and greeted us. I was close to tears, for I hadn't expected to be hospitalized on my first visit to Milwaukee. I was trying hard to adjust.

The girl must have sensed my apprehension. "Hi," she said. "My name is Mary. It really isn't that bad here—you'll get used to it. Where are you from?"

Mary's presence helped to ease my fears. I'd made my first friend at Presbyterian Hospital.

The New Program

My first days on Three South came as a relief to me. I had been struggling as an outpatient for two years, and had sunk to the depths of despair. Now I was finally in a place where someone would help me. I was eager to jump into the program, get better, and go home. I wouldn't learn until much later that the only person who could help me was myself.

The schedule on Three South was quite strict, and it took me a while to get used to it. Our day started early in the morning with a weight check by the nurse on duty. After dressing and brushing our teeth, we were ushered to the dayroom, where we sat and awaited breakfast.

Mealtimes at the Eating Disorders Unit were quite an experience. One eating-disordered person at the dining room table is more than enough. A whole roomful of eating-disordered people makes for a really dysfunctional dining experience.

At mealtimes, both the adult and the adolescent Three South units came together to eat in one dining room. Our meals were supervised by the nursing staff and timed; we had exactly one half hour for meals and fifteen minutes for snacks. What was not eaten during mealtimes was replaced with the caloric supplement Ensure after meals. We had fifteen minutes to drink the Ensure, or rumor had it that we'd be "tubed" (tube-fed). A typical dinner-table conversation was filled with complaints about portion sizes and other mistakes made on our trays. I hated mealtimes.

After meals, we were ushered back to the dayroom to complete our watch periods. The adults and adolescents had different dayrooms, so we young people returned to our side of the hallway. During watch time, we were supervised so that we couldn't engage in exercise or purgative behaviors. The scheduled watch times were individualized to a patient's privilege level. Some kids had a fifteen-minute watch period, while others had two hours.

We ate six times a day: three meals and three snacks. By the time the two-hour watch period was completed, it was time to eat again. I had a two-hour watch period after meals for my entire stay on Three South.

In the evening we took showers, supervised by Richard, a male nurse. The supervised shower was a humiliating experience for me.

I didn't like undressing in front of myself, much less there in the shower with its see-through curtain, in front of a man. Don't ask me how they decided to pick a male nurse for this task. We had an occasional male patient on our unit, but for the most part the Three South patients were young females. We were all adolescents with a poor body image and shaky self-esteem, and the shower arrangement only made us feel worse.

Once we finished our showers, it was bedtime.

The Nurses of Three South

I was on the "total dayroom" privilege level, which meant that I had to sleep in the dayroom on a cot, in front of the nurses' station. All the new patients, as well as those who were noncompliant or severely underweight, were placed on the total dayroom list. The close level of observation made vomiting, hiding food, and sneaking exercise impossible. The nurses ran a tight ship.

Upon my admission to the unit, I was assigned both a primary nurse and an associate. Joan, a young woman with wavy blonde hair, coke-bottle glasses, and a lisp, was my primary nurse. I got into frequent power struggles with her over my use of the telephone, because Joan didn't like me calling my mother. I used to call home daily in tears, saying, "Mom, you have to come and pick me up. I promise that I'll gain weight. I'll do whatever you want—I promise. You don't know what it's like. I hate it here!" According to Joan, my daily outbursts were disturbing to the other patients. I didn't like having her listen in on my conversations.

Karen, a tall, slim woman with straight blonde hair that flowed down the length of her back, was assigned as my associate nurse. She was an outdoorsy, nature-loving person. I could picture her mountain biking or backpacking in the high Sierras. Karen was much more relaxed than Joan. It was hard to imagine her getting really upset about anything, but before long I saw her temper flare. Only one thing really made Karen upset: the sneaking of exercise. Karen often caught me trying to exercise in my room, and usually punished me by doubling the amount of Ensure I had to drink.

Just as I had done at Memorial Hospital, I entered Dr. Bailey's program fully intending to cooperate. More than anything else, I wanted to get better. I had been miserable for the past several years, and desperately wanted my life to be different. Yet I hadn't been at Presbyterian Hospital long when my motivations changed. I'm not sure just when, but I certainly know the contributing factors.

It didn't take me long to learn that I couldn't do anything right in the eyes of the staff members. Despite my sincere efforts to comply with the program, I was in constant trouble with the nurses.

Mealtimes, as always, were challenging for me. My fear of food and of gaining weight didn't diminish when I entered the hospital. As an outpatient, I had developed elaborate rituals around food. I believed I had to perform these in order to keep myself safe. But during mealtimes on Three South, I wasn't allowed to engage in my ritualistic behaviors. In fact, the nurses who supervised our meals made tactless comments about my eating behaviors, in front of everyone.

On one of my first days at the unit, Joan kept up a running commentary from across the table: "You need to quit cutting that and put it in your mouth . . . No, don't put your fork down between every bite, you need to hold onto it . . . Judy, you're chewing that too many times—you need to swallow it."

My dining experiences on Three South reminded me a lot of the spaghetti incident with my father. I wondered why the nurses didn't wait to discuss my inappropriate behaviors until after the meal, when we were alone. My only recourse was to sit through meals without eating a bite and just drink the Ensure supplement afterwards. I thought this a good compromise, because it saved me the humiliation of being belittled at mealtimes.

I was proud of myself for cooperating as fully as I did. Unfortunately, the staff members were not impressed. To me, my ability to actually drink the Ensure supplement was a big accomplishment (made possible only by the prospect of having a nasogastric tube inserted into my nose). At home, there had been periods when I was afraid to drink anything, including water. I knew my fear was irrational, but that didn't make it go away. I knew water wouldn't make me gain "real" weight, but I also knew that if I drank two eight-ounce cups of it and jumped on the scale, my weight would go up a pound. I used to weigh myself prior to drinking something, and then again afterwards. I used to make myself crazy. Thus, drinking the Ensure with its load of forbidden calories was a giant first step for me.

Nervous Habits

It wasn't long before life in the dayroom began to resemble my life on Station Two North. I wasn't physically locked into the eating disorders unit, but I might as well have been. The rules enforced to keep my behaviors in check were worse than being locked in my room.

Since I was little, I've had some nervous habits. I used to bite my fingernails. I consider this a fairly harmless habit, and it certainly saves on emery boards. Yet Francine, the night nurse, used to yell at me for chewing on my fingernails. She'd walk into the dayroom with a little medicine cup full of Ensure. "Why am I being punished?" I'd ask. "What did I do wrong?" Francine would reply, "You know you're not supposed to bite your nails. I saw you from the window."

I also used to jiggle my foot. Mr. Flanagan had chided me about this, in a fun way. I considered these two habits rather benign, but the nursing staff on Three South didn't agree. One time I was sitting on the sofa, working on a cross-stitch. I must have been inadvertently jiggling my foot. Karen arrived from out of nowhere with a large cup of tepid Ensure, saying "You need to drink this." I looked around to see if she was speaking to someone else. "Me? I need to drink that? Why? What have I done wrong? You can't make me drink that disgusting stuff!" "You know what you did and you need to drink it," Karen retorted. "You were wiggling your foot and I saw you. I know that you were trying to burn calories. You need to drink the Ensure now and quit procrastinating, or I'm going to call Dr. Bailey." Angrily, I drank the supplement.

The nurses were always watching us, waiting for us to do something wrong. I decided that the only way I could keep my feet from jiggling was to sit on them. But this solution to my problem didn't please them, either. I was sitting on the couch with my legs tucked carefully beneath me when Karen appeared with a glass of Ensure, saying, "You need to drink this." "Why? What am I doing wrong now?" "You were doing isometrics," she replied impatiently. "I saw you. You need to drink this now unless you want me to call Dr. Bailey to come up and talk to you." I couldn't believe her unfairness; I wasn't even sure what isometrics were. It didn't matter—I still had to drink the Ensure.

"Life Isn't Fair"

During scheduled watch periods, we were supposed to sit in a particular spot in the dayroom. Once we'd picked the spot we wanted to settle into, we were not to move around until our watch time was completed. This meant we were not allowed to get up and go to the bookshelf to choose a new book, or stand up to get a tissue out of the box on the table. It was worse than being locked in my room. At least when I was alone in my room on Station Two North, I could move around as I pleased, and I didn't have staff members constantly watching me with their critical eyes.

I remember thinking that life on the Eating Disorders Unit wasn't fair. While I was growing up, my mother had always told me, "Life isn't fair." Now I knew she was right. Sometimes the nurses would just come up to us and take our pulse, on the theory that they'd be able to tell if we'd been exercising by an increase in our heart rate. Most of the time, I hadn't been doing anything to warrant their suspicion. The nurses' mere presence was enough to boost my anxiety level and increase my heart rate. I was often made to drink Ensure because of such incidents.

The staff members had their own vocabulary, which I quickly assimilated into my own. Extra Ensure supplement, used for punishment purposes, came to be called "a replacement." The staff used to threaten us by saying, "If you don't watch out, I'll replace you." Replacements often came without reason, without warning, and without explanation. I was frequently "replaced." Sometimes something as silly as dropping your bar of soap too many times in the shower brought a replacement. The nurses considered this to be a form of exercise. I thought the staff members were awfully paranoid, but it didn't matter what I thought. I was just some messed-up adolescent psychiatric patient.

The word "nonissue" was also part of the Three South vernacular. We were not supposed to talk about food, weight, exercise, or anything pertaining to our eating disorders. According to the staff, these were nonissues. I think the nurses wanted to convey the idea that eating and weight were not the real problems. They were certainly right, in that respect. However, a lot of energy was wasted by the equally obsessive focus on nonissues, and the whole idea lost its original purpose. It's impossible to control what is said between patients, but this is what they attempted to do. If we were caught discussing any of the nonissues, we were replaced as a punishment.

The Ensure Incident

For me, the nurses couldn't have come up with a worse punishment than making me drink extra supplement. One memory from my first days on the unit still strikes me as funny. I hadn't eaten my supper, so I had a large Styrofoam cup, filled to the top with Ensure, sitting in front of me. I was scared to drink the fattening formula, and scared not to. I think I just plain panicked. I started pouring the Ensure onto the floor, in small increments, when the staff wasn't looking. The dining room had a brown indoor-outdoor carpet. I thought the formula would just soak into the rug, but I was wrong. It stood there on the carpet in a big bubble.

I thought I was going to die from anxiety. *Now* what was I going to do? Using my feet, I tried to massage the Ensure into the carpet. This tactic worked; the stuff soaked into the carpet (and my socks).

I was about to make a quick, inconspicuous exit from the dining room when Katy (a young bulimic patient) stepped into the wet spot. It might not have been so bad, but she started screaming "Oh, my God!" The staff members ran to her. Katy said she had just stepped into something wet on the floor. The nurses told her it was probably just water, but Katy said, "Oh no, it's like Ensure!" My roommate, Melissa, was sitting across the table trying to contain her laughter. The Ensure incident was only my first in a long series of run-ins with the staff on Three South.

My Friends on the Unit

What was to have been a brief hospital stay turned into an extended sentence. I stayed on the adolescent Eating Disorders Unit for eight months of hell on earth. Fortunately, several of my eating-disordered peers helped to ease my suffering. I met many other young people during my stay, and I was grateful for these friends on the unit. There was a strong camaraderie among us. By now, some of their names and faces have become blurred together in my memory, but I still wonder about many of them and how they're doing. I don't know if the answers would be heartening or disturbing, so I guess I'd really rather not know.

Mary

Mary, who was housed on the adult side, was a mentor to me from day one. She gave me a lot of encouragement and support. Mary had been in her junior year of premed studies at Cornell, working toward a major in biochemistry. At that point in time, I wanted to go to medical school and was considering a biochemistry major. I looked up to Mary. When I grew discouraged and depressed, she used to tell me, "Life will get better. You just have to believe it."

Mary seemed to be doing well on the unit. She was one of Dr. Bailey's model patients. She told me that gaining weight wasn't so bad, and that I would get used to it as she had. Unfortunately, appearances can be deceiving. Maybe Mary was really just trying to convince herself, because several years later she died of starvation. I saw her not long before her death. Mary's health insurance had been completely exhausted by her lengthy hospitalizations. At a height of five feet, seven inches, she weighed only fifty pounds.

Melissa

I'm not telling these stories to paint a depressing picture, but to convey a realistic impression of anorexia and other eating disorders. These accounts are not fictitious. They're the real stories of my former friends from treatment. Fortunately, my own story has a happy ending. I was never one to give up easily; I've always been a fighter. It was my fighting spirit that brought me through the battle with anorexia in one piece.

My roommate was a short girl with long brown hair and a solemn face. Melissa was thirteen and looked younger. She, too, was a fighter. This was not her first hospitalization; she'd been on Three South before and had come back again. Melissa was what I would call a hard-core anorexic. She was well-versed in hospital etiquette, but not a model patient like Allison. She had been on the unit for quite some time with few privileges. Melissa was always getting into trouble with the staff members. I couldn't understand why she was so rebellious, and didn't like being around her.

But in time, Melissa and I became the best of friends. We were war buddies. I grew to understand and appreciate her view of the mental-health system. My friendship with Melissa helped pull me through some of my most difficult moments. With her insider's understanding of what I was going through, Melissa was always there to support me, and I was there for her, too. I'm happy to say that today both Melissa and I have fully recovered and are leading fulfilling lives. We continue to be close friends.

Julie

Julie was a young dietetics student who had been attending the University of Wisconsin at Green Bay. She was tall, with medium-length brown hair, cheeks swollen from vomiting, and shoulder bones that protruded through her clothing. Her glasses looked too large for her face.

Julie slid easily through the program. She cooperated just to gain her freedom and go back to anorexia. She would whisper to me, "I can't wait to get out of here. I'm going to lose so much weight. Do you know that I have laxatives hidden in my room?" I knew that Julie got away with a lot of things that the staff never found out about. Of course, she was only hurting herself. I've kept in occasional contact with Julie and feel sad to say that, more than ten years later, she is still struggling with her illness.

Laura

Then there was Laura, a little waif of a thing with her angular body and wisps of blonde hair. At thirty, she had been anorexic for two-thirds of her life. I often wondered why she was so quiet; she seemed to fade into the woodwork in a subconscious wish to disappear. Laura was very cooperative with the program and made few waves. She knew the system all too well.

I am sad to say that Laura is now deceased. Twenty years of severe anorexic and bulimic illness wreak havoc on a person's body. Prolonged laxative abuse and vomiting had left her without a functioning bowel. When I knew her, she had a colostomy, a surgically created opening that drained stool into a bag she wore on her side. Eventually, Laura's body gave out and her heart stopped.

Kelly

Kelly was the daughter of a well-known professional football coach. She was a very tall girl, which only accentuated her gaunt appearance. She had been attending college at the University of Wisconsin. Kelly sailed through the program with what looked like relative ease. She was very sneaky and got away with a lot. I was always upset when I found her vomiting in my wastebasket. I ended up taking the punishment, while she walked away. On her passes, Kelly used to buy a stockpile of laxatives, just to be on the safe side. She was always sick. Her excuse was that her food didn't agree with her. I knew the truth: it was the laxatives.

I don't know what ever became of Kelly, or whether she is still alive today. Based on her predischarge behavior, I know that she couldn't have had an easy time once she returned home.

Joshua

One of the few males on the unit was Joshua, a pathetically thin boy of about eleven with dark brown hair. It was all too obvious that he delighted in his thinness. The competitiveness that exists among people with eating disorders was a central part of his life. Joshua used to walk up with a big grin on his face and wrap his fingers around my arm like a measuring tape, saying, "Judy, you're so thin." I understood his implied message: "Ha ha. I'm thinner than you are." I shrugged him off with a "Leave me alone and don't touch me."

I had a love/hate relationship with Joshua. I loved him during his sensitive, sane moments, and hated him when he was being sick and manipulative. Joshua was abandoned by his biological father when he was young, and he never got over it. He carried a weathered-looking picture of his father with him everywhere. Joshua had lived with his mother and stepfather, and the stepfather had molested him for years. Joshua never talked about this, but I knew about it through certain references that he made.

Joshua was sly. I'll never forget the time he sat on his pudding at the dinner table, to get out of eating it. I don't know how he thought he was going to get up from the table without anyone noticing. He looked so funny, it was all I could do to keep from laughing.

Other things that Joshua used to do were not so funny. He would vomit in blankets in the dayroom, or run away from the unit to buy laxatives. Like Kelly, Joshua got away with many hidden behaviors. Dr. Bailey really liked him. In his eyes, Joshua could do no wrong. All these years later, Joshua is still unwell. The last time I heard about him, he was being transferred to a more secure facility following a suicide attempt.

5

Doing Battle With
Dr. Bailey

My experience on Three South wasn't completely negative. In fact, some of the best moments of my adolescence occurred on the Eating Disorders Unit.

I've always had a pretty good sense of humor, which I probably got from my father. My conservative, professorial dad likes to play practical jokes. He does things like wear a fake nose to class to get a laugh from his students. He'll do something goofy without even cracking a smile. I, too, have the practical-joker gene.

At the hospital, Melissa became my partner in crime. Our pranks started soon after I realized how pointless it was trying to please Dr. Bailey or any of the other staff members. The nurses, like Bailey, were utterly serious. As time went by, their inability to laugh only made our jokes more fun.

"The Big Bee"

Melissa and I devised a number of nicknames for Dr. Bailey, whom we had come to strongly dislike. Our favorites included "The Bailmonster," "God: The Man," and "The Big Bee." It was my idea to draw a big bumblebee on the chalkboard in the day-room. I drew a large stinger on it and wrote "The Big Bee" underneath it. The bumblebee was a depiction of Dr. Bailey and was meant to make a mockery of him. We thought it was quite funny when the doctor failed to comment on it during his morning rounds, missing the obvious symbolism. I'm sure Dr. Bailey never figured it out. If he had, Melissa and I would have been punished.

Dr. Bailey was short-statured—probably even shorter than I am. It seemed to me that he had a short man's complex. One thing was for sure: Dr. Bailey loved to be in power and expected everyone around him to do exactly as he said. After all, he was the person who wrote all the orders on the unit. Dr. Bailey made morning rounds each weekday. We could hear him coming, because of the way he slid his shoes down the hallway. Melissa and I coined the phrase "the Bailey shuffle" to describe the sound he made. We'd whisper to each other, "Uh oh, I hear the Bailey Shuffle."

My Journal

Melissa and I both kept extensive journals. My typical journal entry began with the date, followed by my morning weight. How I weighed in was a good indicator of how the day would go for me. If my weight were up, it would be a bad day. If it were down, the day would be better. The remainder of my daily log consisted of a summary of all the things that happened to me that day, and how I felt about them.

I used to write down all the mean things the staff members said. Dr. Bailey often told me I was a snotty brat. In any other medical setting, this language would be considered inappropriate, even abusive. Yet, for reasons that still elude me, Dr. Bailey got away with such remarks. For their part, the nurses used to tell me, "You're just state hospital material. You're going to end up in some state hospital somewhere." Probably they wanted to scare me out of my illness, but their statements only caused me pain.

Dr. Bailey had a way of charming the parents and then treating the patients poorly. My daily encounters with him were anything but friendly. For one thing, he always called me by my last name. I didn't like being addressed this way; it was disrespectful. I had a first name—Judy—but according to Dr. Bailey my name was Sargent.

To him I was just Bed Number 3135, the seventeen-year-old anorexic.

Most people have no idea what it's like to be trapped in the mental-health system. You become just another name, another number, another clinical diagnosis. Your unique identity gets lost in all the medical jargon. In the eyes of the typical staff member, the individual becomes his or her illness.

Health professionals need to look beyond the disease or disorder. They need to focus on a patient's inner strength, to encourage the positive, to believe in an individual's ability to heal. I wish that Dr. Bailey and the nurses could have seen and encouraged my many strengths.

While I was on Three South, I went through the first of what would be a series of commitment hearings. That first hearing dramatically changed my life. I was no longer a legal adult, free to make my own choices, but a committed psychiatric patient, with no say in the matter. I was declared mentally incompetent, whatever that's supposed to mean. They say that you have to be a danger either to yourself or to someone else. I didn't think I was a danger to myself, and I knew I wasn't a danger to anyone else—except maybe Dr. Bailey, because I might drive him to do something he'd later regret.

At least I always had my journal. The staff members could control what I ate and they could watch me in the shower, but they couldn't control what I wrote about them or how I felt about what went on in my life. For these reasons, my journal was an important outlet for me.

An Enforced Separation

The staff on Three South began to keep Melissa and me apart—physically, since they couldn't separate us emotionally. We were no longer allowed to sit on the same side of the dayroom or to eat next to each other at the dinner table. I was moved to a different room. The nurses offered no explanation as to why they were separating us, but Melissa and I thought we knew.

Melissa came from a family of highly conservative Quakers. Her parents believed it was a grave sin for her to cut her hair, watch television, listen to music on the radio, or wear anything other than a dress. I had given her a sweatshirt and a pair of sweatpants. Her parents had found the forbidden items while snooping through her drawers during a visit, so Melissa and I assumed that they were behind our separation. Whatever the reason for the separation, my best support was being taken away from me. I wouldn't let that happen without a fight.

Melissa and I developed creative ways to stay in close contact. We managed to swap journals and exchange notes. We had two notebooks that were in use at all times. We each wrote in both of the notebooks. We didn't write anything that would identify the one who had written it. We used to leave one of the notebooks in a place where the other of us would find it and pick it up as her own. One time, Melissa slid a notebook down the hallway to me. When one of the nurses caught her in the act, Melissa said she had accidentally dropped the notebook. The nurse actually believed her.

Although the staff was suspicious of our activities, only Theresa ever found out what we were up to. Theresa, a young woman with sandy brown curls, was our favorite nurse. She didn't like Dr. Bailey, and she thought many of the rules were dumb. She used to help us slip our notebooks back and forth, and she stretched other rules for us as well.

Staying in Touch

Once Melissa went out on a pass and smuggled some walkie-talkies back in with her. Of course these toys were forbidden, since she and I weren't supposed to interact. But we had great fun with the walkie-talkies until they were discovered and confiscated. I remember hiding under my covers at night and talking to Melissa in her room: "Ten-four. Smoky, do you read me?"

To thwart the staff's attempts to separate us, Melissa and I were often the last ones at the dining room table. We drank many Ensure cocktails together. Sometimes the hospital was out of Ensure and we had to drink Osmolite or Enrich. Osmolite was never meant to be consumed as a drink. It was intended for tube feedings. It tastes like crushed vitamins. Even worse than the Osmolite was Enrich, which tasted like Ensure, only with ground-up balls of lint mixed in. The label on the Enrich package said that it was "enriched" with fiber. Melissa and I were certain that the formula contained lint balls off of someone's socks.

A Kite for Francine

Melissa and I found ways to continue, and even improve upon, our practical jokes. Any type of belt, cord, or string was forbidden on the unit. The staff thought we might use it to strangle ourselves (or perhaps them). One day, though, Melissa's visiting sister brought us some kite string. Melissa and I were thrilled to have the forbidden string in our possession. We crayoned a big kite on a large sheet of construction paper. We made it in ugly colors (brown and black) and taped a note to it for the mean night nurse, Francine.

We were always in trouble with Francine, even when we hadn't done anything wrong. She used to fill medicine cups with Ensure and sneak up out of nowhere to scold us for bad behavior, such as turning over in our sleep on the cots in front of the nurses' station. According to Francine, we were always trying to burn calories. She reminded me of the Wicked Witch of the West.

That afternoon, we ran the kite string down the length of both units, along the wall. Melissa was allowed to sleep in her room that night; I was still sleeping in the dayroom. As we had planned, Melissa waited until midnight and then began reeling in the kite string until the kite came down the hallway to the nurses' station. The card on top read, "Good Morning, Francine."

We expected to get into a lot of trouble. Instead, Francine loved the kite and thanked us profusely for it. Her response only made our prank more fun. Didn't she know it was supposed to be ugly? Francine told us she was going to take the kite home and put it up on her wall. I wonder if it's still there today.

The Vaseline Caper

Melissa and I played pranks of all kinds, but my favorite one of all was the Vaseline caper.

Because my lips were always dry, my mother had brought me a big jar of Vaseline. One evening Melissa and I were bored, and looking for some kind of joke to play on the staff. The doors to the patient rooms on our unit had no doorknobs. Instead, they had large metal moldings that you had to put your hand up into in order to open the door. I told Melissa, "I have a great idea. Let's go down both hallways and place a small glob of Vaseline up inside each molding. When the staff reach their hands up into the moldings, it'll feel like snot. Just imagine the looks on their faces!"

When we carried out this marvelous plan, Dr. Bailey had a fit. He called my mother at work and told her what we had done. Mom told Dr. Bailey to get himself a sense of humor, but Melissa and I got in a lot of trouble. Dr. Bailey came shuffling up to the unit and yelled at us, his eyes glowering, his face beet red. We were sent to our respective rooms to think about things, and were each made to drink a large Styrofoam cup full of the dreaded Ensure supplement. I didn't mind the punishment. The fun we'd had was worth it.

Rebelling in Earnest

When Christmas came, nearly everyone received some type of pass away from the unit for the holiday . . . everyone but me. I just barely missed my weight requirement for the privilege. To get a pass, I was supposed to weigh ninety pounds, and I weighed in at eighty-nine and a half pounds (with no tricks involved). I had been on the unit for several months, and they wouldn't even give me a two-hour pass on Christmas Day. I hadn't been outside in months, and I longed for a breath of fresh air. Many of the kids got forty-eight or seventy-two hour passes to go home; I didn't think I was asking for much.

I spent Christmas day watching snowflakes fall and staring from the window at passing cars, waiting for Mom and Bobby to arrive from Minneapolis. Bobby had been released from the residential care center, and my mother had placed him in a group home in Minneapolis. This would be only my third time seeing him since the day he left home, but from now on I'd be able to see him more often. Nearly thirteen years had elapsed, and we were now seventeen.

Bobby and my mother arrived loaded with bundles of Christmas gifts. We spent the day on the unit, Mom and I watching Bobby wander from room to room and trying to keep him out of trouble. Bobby sensed my pain that day. He looked directly at me and commented, "You are not going to cry." Maybe we hadn't lost our connection, that special language known only to twins.

The new year began, and then came my eighteenth birthday. I didn't get a pass on those occasions, either. Dr. Bailey was not happy that I was merely drinking the Ensure. He wanted me to be eating the food, so he refused to give me a pass.

"You'll get a pass only when you demonstrate to us that you're able to eat," he pronounced.

"I'm gaining weight—what more do you want?" I snapped. "Who cares whether I eat or drink that nasty supplement? Either way, I'm gaining weight!" As usual, Dr. Bailey ignored my argument. It was then that I decided to retaliate.

My grand rebellion began shortly after I turned eighteen. The withholding of a pass on my birthday had been the last straw. I couldn't please Dr. Bailey if I stood on my head and drank Ensure through my toes. If Dr. Bailey had thought I was noncompliant before, now I was going to show him some real noncompliance!

Several days after my birthday, Dr. Bailey went out of town for a couple of days. This was a perfect time to begin my rebellion, because I wouldn't have to face repercussions from Dr. Bailey until he got back. While he was away, I didn't eat and I didn't drink the Ensure. When Dr. Bailey returned, I was in a world of trouble. He was furious that I had dared to cross him, and demanded that I drink enough supplement to make up for the entire time he'd been away.

My First Tube Feeding

I was not about to comply with Dr. Bailey's demands. I sat at the dining room table and firmly refused to drink the Ensure. It was a matter of principle, and I wasn't going to back down. Dr. Bailey threatened me with a large-bore, clear-plastic naso-gastric tube, setting it out on the table to scare me. His threats didn't faze me. Whatever happened, I needed to be able to live with myself, and I wasn't about to give in. The man was only strengthening my determination.

The doctor stood above me, yelling, "You're going to drink it, God damn it!" *Oh no I'm not, and you can't make me,* I thought. He told me to drop my head back in preparation for the insertion. He seemed to be trying to kill my spirit once and for all. *No way in hell am I going to do what you say,* I thought. Finally Dr. Bailey grabbed me by my hair, yanked back my head, and rammed the tube down my nose. The device hurt really badly going down, and made me choke. The physical pain caused my eyes to water, but it wasn't nearly as bad as the emotional pain.

Dr. Bailey pulled the tube back up and rammed it down again, saying, "I'm going to keep on doing this until you drink it!" From that moment on, I was convinced that he harbored only ill will for me. This was the same person who had told me, only two months earlier, "I will make you well." Was this what he had meant? Now I would rather have died than drink the supplement. I would never let Dr. Bailey manipulate me with his torture. Never.

Eventually, I was tube-fed the supplement, but I had won the battle of wills with Dr. Bailey.

* * *

Six "Meals" a Day

My refusal to eat and drink didn't end with the tube-feeding crisis. It was still a matter of principle, and I wasn't going to give in to their manipulations. So I was tube-fed in a similar manner over the next several weeks, six times a day. Dr. Bailey must have gotten nervous about the many tube insertions, because all of a sudden I started having blood work done every day. I didn't know what they were drawing my blood for, but I knew they were worried about something. One of the nurses told me that my levels were falling.

As an eighteen-year-old anorexic, the battle of wills with Dr. Bailey was my primary concern. Now that I'm on the other side of the line, so to speak, in my career as a registered nurse, I want to make public the unspeakable damage inflicted upon me at that time. I now know that the hospital must have been watching my serial hemoglobin and hematocrits, which will fall if a person is internally bleeding.

After several days of the tube feedings, I was taken to have an endoscopy performed. Dr. Bailey and his staff had ruptured my esophagus with their punitive tube feedings. When I returned to the floor, I was placed on peripheral parenteral nutrition, an intravenous form of nutritional support. Dr. Bailey wanted me to have a Hickman Catheter, a central intravenous line into the superior vena cava of my heart, surgically placed. He needed my mother to sign the consent form, but she refused because of the risk of infection with the catheter. Eventually, a small-bore Dobhoff tube (a type of nasogastric tube) was put in place, and I was fed that way.

I continued to call my mother daily, crying out, "Mom, you have to help me! You have to come get me and take me home." My poor mother didn't know what to do. She called Dr. Bailey to ask about taking me home. He told her, "If you take her home now, she's going to die. Her liver-function test is grossly abnormal. You don't want her to die, do you?" My mother called me back to try to comfort me, saying, "It's just going to be a little bit longer, honey. You need to hang in there. Dr. Bailey says you're not ready to come home."

I didn't tolerate the tube feedings well. The Ensure formula sat in my stomach, made me feel nauseated, and gave me diarrhea. So Dr. Bailey prescribed Reglan, a horrible-tasting orange medicine used to enhance digestion. I had a bad reaction to the drug. It was miserable. I lost control of all my facial muscles, especially my tongue. It was as if my entire face were in one big spasm. The reaction was very painful. It felt as if someone were ripping my tongue out of my mouth. My neck was twisted to one side; my eyes were rolled up into my head. I looked like a complete spastic freak— not good for someone so concerned with her appearance! Dr. Bailey let me endure the reaction and did nothing to help me. It took several hours for the drug to wear off and my symptoms to subside. I was convinced that Dr. Bailey liked to see me suffer.

Because the Reglan failed to work for me, Dr. Bailey was forced to let me take brief jaunts in the hallway, several times daily. He wasn't pleased about letting me walk around, because this violated his exercise taboo. My ability to get around his exercise restriction was a big win for me, in my mind. When I heard the Bailey shuffle, and I was up and walking in the hallway, I used to pick up my pace just to irritate him. My efforts were successful . . . I always managed to bug him. I would ram my stupid i-med pole down the hallway in front of me with the tube-feeding setup, avoiding my doctor's critical glances. On several occasions Dr. Bailey threatened to take away my walking privilege. I remember thinking, *Fine. Go ahead and do that and see if I care. Then you won't be able to run the tube feeding at such a fast rate, and I won't gain weight so fast.*

By this time, my mother was convinced that the program wasn't helping me. However, Dr. Bailey and the nursing staff undertook commitment proceedings to keep me from leaving the hospital against medical advice. Mom hired a lawyer to represent me and attended the hearing with me. The lawyer said, "I think we have a pretty good chance of winning this case." But Dr. Bailey told the court, "If she doesn't stay in the program, she'll die," and thus succeeded in keeping me a prisoner of his program.

Two Great Escapes

I ran away from the unit twice, in protest. Melissa smuggled clothes to me for my first escape: a yellow sweat suit and pink flowered socks, but no shoes. I exited down the back stairwell in my socks. My great escape wasn't really an attempt to run away. I just wanted to get some fresh air. I went back on my own after several hours. When I returned to the unit, I was placed on "elopement precautions." The resulting close observation level made my second escape an even greater feat.

The second time I ran away, I took along a girl named Jennifer who was on the unit for obesity. Jennifer was always talking about running away, but I don't think she really meant it. One day I told her, "Okay, if you really want to run from the unit, let's go." Despite her protestations, I dragged her down the back stairwell.

We had a lot of fun that day. We went for a long walk around a beautiful lake in our socks. There were sailboats on the lake, a soft breeze was blowing, and it was nice and warm. I think Jennifer had fun; I know I did.

Tied to My Bed

I wasn't about to give in to the staff's manipulations and drink the Ensure, nor was I going to passively accept the tube feedings. Thus, it wasn't long before they tied me to my bed in four-point restraints, in an attempt to keep me from pulling out my NG (naso-gastric tube). It was a futile attempt. I used to bite through the tube to register my protest. I found clever ways to get hold of the tube, despite my limb restraints, and spent many a night in sheets soaked with cold Ensure or Osmolite.

Today, the smell of either formula is almost enough to make me vomit. When I prepare tube-feeding formula at work, I'm careful to avoid the aroma with its unpleasant memories. I'm also sensitive to how the patients feel about being force-fed this awful stuff.

The physical restraints were uncomfortable. I used to pull against them till my hands turned blue. I did this to annoy the staff and show them that I wasn't going to give in without a fight. Then I did sit-ups, just to bother them further. This was foolish, for it only resulted in the restrictiveness of my restraints being increased.

I could sense that my behavior was not well received by a number of the nurses. I'm sure that, when they made out the shift assignments, I was the last patient to be selected. I was what the staff considered a problem patient. Several months into my stay, my primary and associate nurses asked to be taken off of my case. This felt like a real letdown; I gathered that they had just given up on me.

During this time, I saw a clinical psychologist named David Jones. He was a balding, middle-aged man with an affinity for polo shirts. At first I was happy not to have to talk with Dr. Holland anymore. I figured that any change had to be a positive one. David was a mild-mannered person, and I didn't mind seeing him. But after a while I realized that he and Dr. Bailey talked behind the scenes. I also learned that the professional principle of holding client information in confidence meant nothing to David.

Talking to David—or to any of the nursing staff, for that matter—was like broadcasting your feelings over the evening news. I learned that I couldn't talk to them about the things that concerned me unless I wanted the whole unit to know. Apparently, bits and pieces from my sessions were recorded in my chart. On more than one occasion, a staff member remarked to me, "I heard that you . . ." I remember thinking, *How did you hear that, because I never told you—and wouldn't have chosen to, either!*

I learned that I had to be more quiet about my feelings. Accordingly, I spent many of my sessions complaining about trivial things like my weight, the food, the mean nursing staff, and especially how I hated Dr. Bailey. *Fine, break my confidence. Go tell that to Dr. Bailey! See if I care.* Being a psychiatric patient is like being stripped naked and placed onto a podium where everyone can scrutinize you for your faults, inch by inch. I would no longer give them anything real to scrutinize.

Depression

The months I spent tied to my bed in four-point restraints were some of my darkest times ever. I remember lying there and thinking that death might be a more desirable option. Not surprisingly, I added a new diagnosis to my list, becoming what the professionals describe as clinically depressed. The depression that overcame me permeated my being and darkened all my perceptions. It was as if I were looking at the world through hazy dark glasses. A shadow had been cast, and in it the whole world looked gloomy. I knew I didn't want to die, but I didn't want to live like that, either.

The staff's solution to my new problem was to call in a psychiatrist to prescribe an antidepressant for me. I was angry at them for trying to medicate me out of my misery, trying to reduce my behavior to some chemical imbalance. The way I was being treated on the unit was the source of my depression. Medication would never change that, and I certainly wasn't going to take it. So they sent the antidepressant down my feeding tube. Not surprisingly, it did nothing to elevate my mood.

Tony

During the months I spent tied to my bed, only my friends could ease my depression. Tony, who was about my age, with a huge frame, dark brown hair, and a smart mouth, was one such friend. Tony was on the unit to lose weight. I always admired the way he stood up to Dr. Bailey, fearlessly confronting him with his complaints. Tony and I became immediate friends. He was my friend, my confidant, my best advocate. He more than once stood up for me, saying, "You know, Dr. Bailey, it's really not fair what you're doing to Judy." Tony's popularity rating among the staff was about as low as mine. We made a great pair.

After I was confined to my room and tied to my bed, Tony used to sneak in to talk to me. The door would fly open, then close again just as quickly, and a deep voice would say, "Whew, that was close. I almost got caught." I spent countless afternoons crying on Tony's shoulder. He sat at my bedside, holding my hand and comforting me. I don't know what I would have done without Tony.

Barb and Theresa

My new primary and associate nurses, Barb and Theresa, also proved to be a blessing for me. Both had faith in my ability to recover. Barb was a seasoned nurse with black hair, glasses, and a wonderful sense of humor. She often used humor to engage my attention and enlist my cooperation. I still have one of the lists she made me complete as a homework assignment, titled "Judy's S.O.S. (for same old shit) List." I was supposed to write down all my eating-disordered behaviors. Barb started the list for me: "I know I'm in S.O.S. mode when I run until my feet bleed, and it ain't the shoes." Barb could always make me laugh, even when things were hard.

Theresa, although she had a more refined sense of humor, was equally compassionate. She was empathetic to my pain, fears, and struggles, and she never put me down. She even sat in the day-room and schemed with us about what we should do to Dr. Bailey, and helped us think up funny practical jokes. I recall her saying, "Oh, you guys are so bad to think of something like that. You know Dr. Bailey wouldn't think that was funny. You'd better not try it, but it's a great idea. You might try *this*, though, because he would never know." Unfortunately, Theresa resigned shortly after becoming my new associate nurse. She told me she was leaving because she didn't like what Dr. Bailey was doing, and didn't want to be a part of it any more. I understood her reasons for leaving and admired her ability to stand up for her own beliefs. Yet I missed her presence in my daily life on Three South.

A Graduation and a Discharge

My war with Dr. Bailey continued for another couple of months, until my release from the hospital. I wasn't about to give up my insurrection against the man who had betrayed my trust and tortured me.

I wasn't discharged from the unit in the way that most of Dr. Bailey's patients were. The doctor made an agreement with me that, if I ate actual food for three days, he would let me out. He wanted to be rid of me just as much as I wanted to get away from him. I understood his offer to be a business agreement. My acceptance of his terms didn't mean that I had to back down from my stand; it was just a mutual working agreement that would benefit both of us. I was still tube-fed until three days before my release from the hospital.

Thanks to Dr. Bailey, I never attended my own high school graduation. Despite the fact that my weight was at a noncritical level, he refused to write a pass so that I could attend the ceremony. I graduated at the very top of my class, yet my mother had to go to my graduation alone to pick up my honors for me.

I fulfilled the business agreement that I had made with Dr. Bailey, and was released from Presbyterian Hospital in late June of 1986, several weeks after my high school graduation.

6

The Long Road

My freedom from Dr. Bailey and the eating-disorders program came as a great relief, but I was in no way out of the woods. My obsessive desire for perfect thinness had only grown stronger during my eight-month stay on Unit Three South.

I returned home to Minneapolis to live with my mother. While I was away, my father had accepted a research position at Stanford, and my sister had gone to live with him. I missed her, but I had become accustomed to loss. Besides, Anne and I had grown apart in the years since my anorexia had set in. We had little in common anymore, since I avoided all social situations and anything that had to do with food.

Life Back at Home

My mother and I were home alone. We often fought—over my weight, my level of exercise, what I was going to eat—all my "buttons." Before the anorexia, my mother and I had gotten along well. She considered me the perfect child. I had been named after my mother; perhaps she thought of me as a second self and subconsciously lived through me. Then things had changed. All of a sudden, I had become the family's black sheep.

Now, because I hated conflict, I avoided my mother and stayed in my room. I spent most days lying in my heated waterbed, trying to stay warm between manic sprees of exercise. Ashamed of my diagnosis, I didn't call my old high school friends. My loneliness grew. My father was ashamed of me and would no longer acknowledge my existence. What would his colleagues think if they knew that Tom Sargent had a mentally ill daughter?

The one person with whom I still felt a connection was Melissa. She had been discharged from Dr. Bailey's program to a foster home, where she lost weight and stopped drinking fluids. She eventually had to be placed in the state mental hospital. My heart ached for her, as I could imagine what it must be like in that cold, desolate place. Yet we continued to exchange letters. As I wrote, I shared tales of my daily struggles, details of arguments with my mother, a rare conversation with my dad or sister—whatever was going on in my head. In her letters, Melissa shared with me in the same way. Every day when the mailman arrived, I was there to greet him as I eagerly awaited another letter from Melissa.

Up to My Old Tricks

Outwardly, I looked as if I had recovered from the anorexia, because I had gained a lot of weight (nearly thirty-five pounds). Inwardly, I was miserable—and frantic to lose the hated thirty-some pounds. As my desperation increased, I sought out ever more dramatic weight-loss methods.

One afternoon, I found the old bottle of ipecac that we had kept in our medicine chest since I was a child. I was having trouble making myself throw up, and thought the ipecac might help. The liquid in the bottle was purple and foul-smelling. Just drinking the putrid stuff was nearly enough to make me vomit.

I waited. Nothing. I waited some more time. Still nothing. The bottle must have expired in 1970, or maybe I didn't take enough. Either way, it didn't work. Some time later, I got a scare when I read an article describing how ipecac is damaging to the human heart and is never fully eliminated from the body. The article said: "It is little known, but the singer Karen Carpenter actually died from ipecac poisoning." No way would I ever try *that* again.

Yet several weeks later I came up with another bright idea. Remembering how Joshua, Julie, and Kelly had all used laxatives and were all very skinny, I thought, *Maybe I should try taking laxatives.* I walked to the local Quick Trip store to buy a bright blue box of Ex-Lax pills. When I returned home to the privacy of my bedroom, I found that I had actually purchased the chocolate version of Ex-Lax. It resembled a candy bar. *Good*, I thought, *this might not be too bad.* I tasted a square. It tasted so bad, I could hardly choke it down.

The box said: "Take one square daily, as needed." I followed the directions and waited. Nothing. I waited longer. Still nothing. Finally I got impatient and took the whole box. In the middle of the night, I woke up with such a bad case of the runs that I wasn't even sure I could make it to the bathroom. I spent the rest of the night and the whole next day on the toilet. I think I told my mother, "I must have the flu." As I sat there with stomach cramps and a raw butt, I once again vowed, *I'm never doing* that *again.*

After I returned home, a number of people I knew made comments about my weight. They used to come up and say, in a congratulatory way, "You've gained weight." For those of you who don't know, that's not the thing to say to someone who is anorexic. I remember that I felt like crying. I took the comments as confirmation that I was really fat. My mother used to tell me, "They didn't mean it that way." But I didn't care how they meant it. I hated their comments.

Looking back, I know that all those people intended to pay me a compliment, but I was unable to hear their words as such. Here's a word to the wise. I don't know why some people consider it perfectly all right to remark about another person's weight. Prior to my recovery, a statement of that kind would only upset me and leave me depressed, and would encourage me to start planning a rapid weight loss. Regarding the appearance of anyone with an eating disorder, it's best to avoid that subject altogether.

It wasn't long before I had lost the despised thirty-plus pounds. I was exercising like a maniac by jogging as many as twenty miles a day. Toward the end of a two-month period of frantic weight loss, my mother got "a bad feeling" and took me to the hospital.

From Bad to Worse

Looking at the situation today from a clinical perspective, I know that my body was on the verge of collapse due to the rapidity with which I had lost the weight. I was admitted to a medical unit by an internist who had little or no experience with anorexia nervosa. He ordered that I be given a large quantity of intravenous fluids. The first day, I gained nearly ten pounds overnight. My body swelled like a balloon. The low level of protein in my blood caused the IV fluid to spill into my tissues. This happened according to a simple biochemical concept: water follows solute. Low protein (solute) in my blood caused the fluid to leak into my tissues.

In the middle of the second night, I woke up unable to breathe. I had gone into congestive heart failure, so they transferred me to the coronary intensive care unit. There I was: an eighteen-year-old kid in the midst of a group of mature heart patients. I was terrified that I was dying, but I survived.

You'd think the coronary-care experience would have scared me into recovery, but my anorexia persisted. Let me clarify this for you: I was definitely scared by the experience, but was still unable to free myself from the anorexia. Nobody chooses to be miserable. I certainly wouldn't have chosen my situation. I believe that people do the best they can, given their available coping mechanisms, and I was trying to do just that. It would be many more years before my battle with anorexia was won.

My mother later told me that a nurse from the coronary ICU had told her, "I know this is really painful for you. I must warn you that your daughter won't live to be thirty. Even anorexics who recover don't live long. The chronic malnutrition severely weakens the heart." Mom was upset by the nurse's words, and desperate to prove her wrong. She needed to find me a better treatment program, and right away.

This time, I was hospitalized at St. Francis Hospital, on a general adult psychiatric floor with a great many chronically ill psychiatric patients. In order to be placed in a unit like this, you have to be either a danger to yourself or a danger to others, as determined by a psychiatrist. I met the criteria for "a danger to oneself" due to my self-induced starvation and the rapidity with which I had lost the weight.

My time at St. Francis was completely unlike any of my previous hospital stays. I was not at all prepared for this next experience. I was placed on a locked ward among patients who were chronically mentally ill. Nearly everyone on the floor carried the label "schizophrenia" or "bipolar disorder." The new class of patients with whom I was grouped was very different from the adolescents I'd met during my prior hospitalizations. Most of these people had been ill for the greater part of their lives and had little hope of ever getting better. Now that I had joined them, I was in for a truly rude awakening.

A Chronic Anorexic

The staff members at St. Francis were hesitant to deal with me from the very start, as if they were afraid that if they came too close they might catch my affliction. I felt like a leper. I'm a sensitive person, and I could sense their apprehension; it didn't need to be spoken. So I kept to myself most of the time. If the staff had no interest in interacting with me, I didn't feel like trying to prove myself to them.

Anyway, the staff had me figured out from day one. I was the chronic anorexic in Bed 4212. Until then, I hadn't known that you could be chronically anything at the age of eighteen. I didn't think I had lived long enough to be chronic. I guess I was wrong. I had a label on that unit before I ever had a name or a face. Along with my label came a preconceived notion of what I would be like. I would be sneaky and manipulative, just like all anorexics.

You see, an interesting phenomenon occurs in the world of mental health. Mental-health workers almost always have access to individual patients' histories. They at least have summaries of a person's previous hospitalizations and treatment attempts. Many times a nurse, physician, or other mental-health worker will read a patient's chart, including their history, before ever meeting the patient.

I carried with me the stigma of two previous lengthy and unsuccessful hospitalizations, along with several years of failed psychotherapy. To someone merely reading my history, I'm sure I sounded like a hopeless case. In addition to my prior failed hospitalizations, I was known as a "hospital jumper"—a term used to describe a person who doesn't stick to any one mode of therapy (something mental-health professionals hate). This is why the staff members were leery of me from the start. They didn't have to meet me; they only had to read my chart.

The Company of Psychotics

As I walked onto the inpatient adult psychiatric unit, I came upon a dayroom filled with aimlessly wandering individuals. I was overwhelmed by a smoky haze that permeated the unit. Most psychiatric patients are avid smokers.

I don't think anyone could have prepared me for this next hospital experience. Worse than the dingy, smoke-filled environment was the group of patients I had been thrown in with. I found myself locked onto a ward with a whole bunch of hopelessly psychotic individuals. At first I was scared. What would happen if one of these people were to flip out and try to hurt me? Was it safe for me to sleep at night? Eventually I learned that I didn't have to be scared, because most psychiatric patients are completely harmless.

My first days on the unit reminded me of how, when I was a child, my mother would tell me not to stare at unusual people. When I first got to St. Francis, it would have been nearly impossible to follow my mother's advice. I wouldn't have been able to open my eyes at all, because everyone around me was behaving bizarrely. Some patients were talking to nonexistent people; one man thought he was Jesus Christ; another was convinced he was getting messages from the television; one woman walked about with a towel wrapped around her head; another told me that her potato was talking to her.

There wasn't one patient with whom I could hold a halfway normal conversation. Initially, I felt reassured; the others made me feel relatively functional. Yet, after some time, I began to question my own sanity. I wondered how I had ended up in this place. The doctors must have thought I fit into this group of patients, or they wouldn't have placed me here. Was I really as nutty as the rest of these people? I knew that my obsessions and rituals were pretty crazy. Did that make *me* crazy?

Magic Pills

Dr. Clifford Nelson, a distinguished-looking older gentleman, was the physician in charge of my care at St. Francis. Dr. Nelson was a psychiatrist with a specialty in psychopharmacology. Beware of psychopharmacologists! I must have been a great test subject for Dr. Nelson. Had I responded favorably to the multitude of pills he prescribed for me, my story would have made great medical-journal material.

Dr. Nelson was accustomed to prescribing all kinds of antipsychotic medications for his schizophrenic patients. I'll give him credit for creativity. He prescribed a multitude of pills for me to take, in the hope of finding the magic pill that would cure my eating disorder. He once prescribed an antihistamine, only because increased appetite and weight gain were among the side effects. Creative, but no cigar.

The problem was not my appetite. Actually, I was hungry most of the time. I just wouldn't allow myself to eat. The statement "I'm not hungry" makes a great excuse when people are trying to get you to eat.

Dr. Nelson tried his whole repertoire of pills on me, including the antipsychotic medication Thorazine. The pills left me in a drugged fog, and my anorexia remained untouched. When his magic pills failed to work, Dr. Nelson called my mother into his office and gave her his verdict: I was hopelessly schizophrenic. He suggested that I be institutionalized in a state mental hospital. He told Mom that she could save herself time and money, because I'd eventually end up there anyway.

My mother didn't tell me what Dr. Nelson had said until a much later date. I know that his words really rocked Mom's hope for my future. But not only was the doctor's statement untrue, it was potentially very harmful. I hate to think where I'd be today if my mother had followed Dr. Nelson's advice and locked me away in a state hospital somewhere. I was never schizophrenic—not even close. More importantly, my situation was never hopeless.

Any type of meaningful psychotherapy takes time, because real change doesn't occur overnight. The doctors, nurses, and psychologists who treated me were all looking for a quick fix. When their best attempts didn't yield immediate results, many of them proclaimed my situation hopeless. Rather than looking at what parts of the treatment plan were ineffective and sharing some responsibility for the lack of success, they blamed me for the treatment failure and eventually passed my case along to someone else.

During my hospital stay, I saw Dr. Nelson once or twice a week for perhaps ten minutes, fifteen if I was lucky. It was just enough time for me to share with him my dissatisfaction about the food or my physical surroundings. Of course, my real issues were never touched upon. I marvel at Dr. Nelson's clairvoyant ability to determine my future after only a few brief sessions. The staff at St. Francis Hospital never tried to get to know me. Nobody bothered wondering about the Judy who had been preparing to go to an Eastern women's college, Judy with dreams of becoming a medical doctor, Judy the violinist, Judy the person.

*   *   *

More Dark Days

I was eventually released from St. Francis Hospital, and continued to struggle as an outpatient until the time came for my next
hospitalization. Besides seeing numerous therapists, I underwent
endless hospitalizations—twenty-six over a ten-year period. With
all this treatment, the only thing that changed was that I grew
increasingly disillusioned with the mental-health system, and more
hopeless.

I floated between hospitals, therapists, and treatment programs,
trying to find someone with a fresh perspective. I held on to the
hope that I would find some caring individual who could help me.
All my life plans had been put on hold. I didn't think of college
much anymore; I just tried to get through each day. I would never
have actively tried to kill myself, but I often wished that death
would take me in my sleep.

During my long search for someone who could help me, I ran into
a number of ineffectual psychologists and psychiatrists. Each therapist I met had a unique point of view regarding eating disorders
and their proper treatment. I found some of the perspectives humor-
ous and others just plain erroneous, but not one enlightened me.
Despite the fact that many of the psychiatrists had studied for years
to be qualified to treat eating disorders, I found most of them naive
and sadly in the dark when it came to anorexia nervosa.

The Minuchin Model

Several physicians stand out in my memory, such as Dr. Jeffrey
Miller, a psychiatrist who followed the Minuchin school of thought.
The Minuchin model operates on the assumption that the client's
eating disorder is an expression of a larger family dysfunction. It
advocates a "family lunch session" where the whole family is invited
into the therapy session, and the parents are encouraged to make the
anorexic eat. Needless to say, I didn't like this treatment approach

very much. No one would ever make me eat. No one, and least of all my parents!

I think the Minuchin theory has some merits. An eating disorder *is* almost always an expression of a larger family dysfunction. Yet, notwithstanding the existence of underlying family problems, the "family lunch session" is not the answer. I found Dr. Miller's approach amusing. If it were to be a matter of will power, I would certainly win. As far as I was concerned, he was just wasting his energy, but he remained firm in his convictions. Dr. Miller would have had better success with me had he maintained an open perspective.

Overeaters Anonymous

I was also exposed to the Overeaters Anonymous model. This time, the facilities were located in a beautiful country-club-type setting—a nice change from the psychiatric wards I was accustomed to. Each morning we arose and headed straight to the common dayroom. There we recited the OA statement, acknowledging our powerlessness over our illness and reaffirming our commitment to turn our problem over to God.

The only problem was that I hadn't been raised to have faith in God. My father is part Jewish by birth; my mother is Chinese. I was brought up as an agnostic. Was I really powerless over the anorexia? I hoped not. What if I turned my problem over to God and there was no God? The OA model didn't work for me. It requires a firm religious faith, and I hadn't yet stumbled upon the Catholic Church. My faith was still in its infancy.

The Overeaters Anonymous model suggests that a person is never truly freed from the addiction. Individuals are told that they will always have to work to control the impulse to reengage in their problem behaviors. I found that thought quite discouraging. At that time, I was looking for a rapid cure, not a lifelong adjustment process.

Certainly there were parallels between my anorexia and other addictions. Whether you consider an alcoholic, a drug addict, a gambling addict, a sex addict, or an eating-disordered person, the underlying problems are the same. The addictive behavior is just a symptom, a visible sign that something is not right. The alcohol, the weight loss, the drug high, are only ways to cover up painful feelings—to comfort, self-medicate, and numb oneself.

Been There, Done That

In my numerous other hospitalizations, I was placed in private hospitals and public ones, on eating-disorder wards with adolescents, mixed units with both adults and adolescents, and units strictly for adults. I was hospitalized on psychiatric floors with adolescents and children, on wards with adolescents only, and on units where there were only adults. I was placed on locked units and open wards. My mother dragged me from doctor to doctor. I saw psychologists, psychiatrists, medical doctors, dietitians, social workers—anyone who might possibly be able to cure me. I even saw a woman for acupressure. My mother was not going to give up on me.

We went all around the country, trying to find the best treatment center. In her spare time, my mother read books, seeking out information about the various programs, scrutinizing their details, approaches, and philosophies. In time, you lose your will to fight. I had long since become a passive participant in the whole process. I agreed to the intermittent hospitalizations to pacify my mother, more than anything else. I gave up on ever finding anyone who would truly care or be able to help me. Still, I went along with the charade. I told people what they wanted to hear. In order to keep regaining my freedom from the various psychiatric wards, I played the game.

One Last Try

Finally, I was hospitalized on a unit at a large, Midwestern, university-affiliated hospital. The program was and still is very well respected among professionals working in the field. I entered the unit to find myself grouped with a variety of other eating-disordered patients. The unit was located in an old, run-down portion of the hospital building.

We took a rickety elevator up to the fifth floor. Inside the unit, a nurse ushered me to my room for an intake interview. Afterward, I met up with my mother, who was waiting in the hallway. Georgia, the nurse, said, "Make it quick. You have five minutes until lunch. Your mother needs to get going."

I started to cry, telling my mother, "You can't leave me here. This is a mistake. I want to go home." Georgia ushered my mother out through the huge steel door. It slammed shut, and I could hear the lock latch. I knocked on the window behind my mother, shouting, "I hate you! You can't leave me here! Come back and get me! I can't believe that you're just leaving me here!" My mother disappeared into the elevator, turning one last time to look at me, swallowing back her tears. Georgia shook her head at me.

Once in the dining room, I was seated next to Roxanne, another nurse. I could sense the other girls measuring me up, visually weighing me, comparing my arms with theirs, comparing the amount of food on my plate with theirs. It was a silent confrontation, the fiercest of competitions. I sat in front of my tray, which was covered with mounds of food. It held a carton of whole milk, a glass of orange juice, a sandwich laden with mayonnaise, carrot sticks, an apple, and a bowl of ice cream melting in the afternoon sunlight. I peered at the tray and then back at the girls, who were still scrutinizing me from across the table. I couldn't eat—not today. Maybe tomorrow. I stayed at the table and tried to establish my place in the pack. I was like a wolf vying for dominance.

After the meal, Liz, a young bulimic girl, approached me to say, "That was really not cool, what you did in there. A lot of the girls are mad at you. We have to eat, and it's not fair that you can get away with not eating your tray. You'd better wise up and conform, like the rest of us." *Who does she think she is?* I thought. I told Liz, "You don't understand. Just leave me alone."

I didn't make any friends on the unit. I can't blame anyone but myself; I never even tried. After my encounter with Liz, I figured that everyone hated me and there was no point trying. I became increasingly isolated and depressed, and continued to refuse to eat. Eventually, I tried to leave. I went to Georgia and said, "I'd like to leave. Will you bring me the papers so that I can sign myself out against medical advice?" I marvel at my stupidity. The doctors then took me to court and had me legally committed.

Due to my failure to comply with the system, they placed me on a punitive behavior-modification program. I was forced to walk around, day and night, in a hospital gown. I was freezing cold in that scanty outfit. Actually, I was cold all the time, even in summer. What was worse than being so cold was the humiliation I felt having to wear that outfit in front of others on the unit. I was still expected to attend all the daily groups. When visitors arrived in the evening, there I was in my skimpy little gown. If I wasn't careful, the back portion of the gown flew open and exposed my underwear. I'm sure that some visitors asked, "Why is that one girl walking around in her pajamas?" To this, the nurses could sanctimoniously reply, "Because she hasn't complied with the program."

I felt like a child forced to sit in the corner and wear a dunce cap. I never found the punishments motivating. Was I unusual in that respect? I don't think so.

I had been refusing to eat for only two days when the staff decided I should be forcibly tube-fed. In their efforts to convince me to eat, they used the biggest and most uncomfortable nasogastric tube they could find. Georgina and Roxanne held me down on my bed as the doctor forced the garden hose-sized tube down my nose. I screamed and fought with all my might, and as I wrestled with the nurses on the bed, I thought to myself, *That's it. There is no way that I'm going to eat now.*

"When do I get to have the tube taken out?" I asked. Roxanne replied, "Not until you eat. Around here, you need to do what we say. Your behavior is really disturbing to the other girls, but that seems to mean nothing to you. How do you feel about that?" I turned away, silent, and wiped the tears from my eyes.

The large plastic tube I was forced to walk around with was extremely uncomfortable, and it left my throat chronically sore. Yet, once again, I was not about to give in to their manipulations and eat. The guilt trip didn't work, either. I already felt bad enough about myself. I have always been stubborn, and I had made up my mind. I was not going to eat.

I didn't stay on the unit long. I ran away, despite the locked doors and my legal commitment. You see, where there's a will, there's a way. I learned that I could stand by the locked door without being seen. The door had a lag time when closing. I waited until someone passed through the door, and quickly grabbed it before it closed. I was free.

Although my hospitalization was brief, it left a bitter feeling within me. I'm thankful that my mother was willing to come and pick me up after my escape. She realized my desperation and the ineffectiveness of the program. We crossed the state border and stayed in a motel until we had time to formulate a plan and contact a lawyer. I never went back there again.

I know that I share the responsibility for my early treatment failures. By my own behavior, I often rejected the people who were sincerely trying to help me. Looking back, I'm embarrassed by some of the ways I behaved during those years. A lot of my behavior was completely out of keeping with my values and beliefs, and I said a lot of mean and hurtful things to people who didn't deserve it. For that I am sorry.

7

The Lived Experience of Anorexia

When I was underweight, women often approached me to say, "I wish I were anorexic. Can you tell me the secret?" Such women look at the slender bodies of anorexics and figure that they must be happy. From an uninformed viewpoint, the anorexic has achieved the American ideal of a model-thin body. What these women don't know is the real story of the day-to-day experience of anorexia nervosa.

Here are two things in particular that it's important to know: (1) eating disorders are never easy to overcome, and (2) eating-disordered patients need to be treated on an individual basis. What finally worked for me in treatment may not work for someone else. There are no easy answers, and I'm not trying to suggest that I have one. Yet mine was a fairly classical case of anorexia, so I hope my story will give you insight into the lived experience of someone suffering from this disorder.

Self-Improvement

My eating disorder started innocently enough as part of a self-improvement campaign. What was intended to be a simple diet became years of misery and obsession. As I write this, I am not yet thirty. Anorexia has occupied a third of my lifetime, and stolen my youth. I'll be glad if even one person comes away from reading this book with a new perspective, and thereby avoids having to repeat my ordeal.

I never intended to lose control of my diet and my life. It just happened, very subtly and insidiously. The weight loss occurred gradually, and eventually snowballed out of control. I gloried in my thinness; it bolstered my self-esteem. I felt virtuous in my ability to refrain from eating. I measured my own achievement by watching the numbers on the scale. As my weight dropped, I felt better about myself.

Americans, as a society, are obsessed with thinness. Young women pick up popular women's magazines and see emaciated models who have come to represent an unhealthy and unrealistic ideal. Young women in our culture are socialized to believe that thin is beautiful and desirable, that thinness will make them happy. No wonder eating disorders are so prevalent. In order to counteract this tendency, we need to teach young girls to find self-worth through healthier means. We need to take a serious look at our ideals, and work toward instilling self-confidence, independence, and self-esteem in our children.

It's ironic that the very recourse that initially boosted my self-esteem eventually depleted it. Once I had reached a certain state of thinness, people were no longer envious of my achievement, and I received disapproving stares. The negative reactions of complete strangers really shook me, and my self-esteem spiraled downward even further.

Trying to Disappear

Early in my illness, before the first hospitalization, I believed that if I could just hit a certain magical number then I'd be justified in regaining the weight. I fantasized about how medical professionals would nurture me back to health. Unfortunately, I could never find that magical number. As my weight decreased, the thought of gaining any weight at all became increasingly distressing. To the people trying to help me, I denied that there was anything wrong, although inwardly I knew that I was killing myself. As a child, I had sometimes wished I could disappear. Now I was manifesting the wish in a very physical sense. I often felt that I wasn't as good or deserving as others. Other people deserved basic sustenance, but not me. I felt completely justified in my self-denial. In my own mind, I deserved to be punished.

While I was acutely ill, I recall reading just about every eating-disorder book on the market. I read the books in an attempt to find a solution to my problem. What I found was that most of the authors (even the ones I considered the best writers on the topic) mainly described the anorexic's symptoms in needless detail. Some of the authors gave pound-by-pound descriptions of weight loss. Being severely anorexic myself, I became competitive with the characters in the books. It didn't matter whether they were real or fictitious. As I would read, the competitiveness would mount within me as I thought, *I just have to be thinner than her. I need to lose more weight. If she ate only three crackers, I should eat no more than two.* Although some parts of the books might be helpful, my attention was usually distracted by the specific accounts of low weights and by my own desire to be thinner than the characters. My anorexia persisted.

Contributing Factors

Although the illness manifested when I was fifteen, I'm sure that I had all the necessary psychological contributors to anorexia long before then. From early childhood, I had always been a perfectionist and a people pleaser. When my family returned to our old neighborhood after our year in Chicago, I found myself lonely, isolated, and not well accepted by my peers. I was shy and self-conscious, and I didn't wear the popular clothes (a necessary precursor to fitting in). I wanted desperately to be accepted, but my peers considered me a brain and somewhat of a nerd. My self-esteem was damaged; I was frequently the object of teasing.

I was convinced that I was somehow not likable. I went all the way through high school without once being asked on a date. Even the least kind and least intelligent people in school had dates. I took this as evidence that there must be something really wrong with me. I tried to ignore the unkind comments of my school-mates, although inside I was deeply hurt. I used my studies as a means of escape. If I could get perfect grades in school, then I would feel good about myself. Unfortunately, it didn't work that way.

More than anything else, I still wanted to fit in, and I knew that I didn't. I buried myself in solitary pursuits, constantly striving for perfection. I thought perfection would make me happy. If I were perfect, then it wouldn't matter what other people thought of me; I would know I was okay. I got straight A's in school, I took a medal in the state swim competition, I sat third chair in the first violins, and I was still not perfect enough, because I wasn't happy.

Anorexia tends to affect affluent, gifted young women of high intelligence. Looking back, I marvel at my ability to become so completely caught up in an obsession based on false premises and invalid reasoning. The whole disorder started with the belief that *If I were thinner, then I'd be happy. If only I were more perfect, then life would be okay.* In reality, the concepts of "fat" and "skinny" have no relation to true happiness and a meaningful existence. But it took me many years to realize this fact.

Hindsight is always 20/20, they say, and it *is* far easier to see things as they really are when you look back in retrospect. The emotions have lost their immediacy, and you can see the situation more objectively. You may wonder, "How could an intelligent and educated girl come to hold such irrational beliefs and engage in such senseless behavior?" I have many times asked myself, *How did I ever get caught up in such a crazy obsession? Why did I waste more than ten years of my life?* I don't know. I will tell you that the line between mental health and mental illness is not as wide as you may think. Given enough stress or psychological provocation, any one of us might cross it.

*   *   *

Rituals and Obsessions

Throughout my long ordeal, I was acutely aware how irrational my thinking was. This only contributed to my misery. My obsessive thoughts ranged from food and exercise all the way to cleanliness. I often wished I could take a break from my thoughts for even a couple of hours, but they went on unabated.

I spent hours calculating and recalculating calories, getting upset when discrepancies existed between my various calorie books (and they always did). My obsession with calories became even worse during my hospitalizations and times of weight restoration (or "refeeding," as it is called). I was convinced that the dietitians were inaccurate in their calculations. I kept myself busy with all my tabulations, so busy that I didn't have to think about what was really bothering me. The inaccuracy of the dietitians' calculations made tube feedings and supplemental replacements a more desirable option than eating food, despite the naso-gastric tube. Rather than reasoning that dietary calculations are never precise and that the discrepancies would balance out over a several-day period, I stayed stuck in my rigid thinking.

In addition to the thoughts of food, I had numerous exercise obsessions. During my daily jog, I felt compelled to engage in a variety of elaborate rituals. For instance, I'd developed rules about how to turn a corner, how I was supposed to step on and off a curb, and so forth. If I didn't feel I had done it correctly, I had to start all over again and do it right. Even if I initially felt that I'd done it right, I would ruminate over the fact that I just *thought* I had done it correctly when in fact I had done it wrong. At that point, I would go back and do it again. I'm sure this is hard for most people to understand. It never made any sense to me, either.

I had shower rituals, too. Cleanliness was one of my obsessions. I showered several times a day, for an hour or more each time. I used to shower until the water heater ran out of hot water. I had developed rules about how many times I had to twist the soap bar each time I picked it up. I went through great quantities of soap, and my skin looked like a lizard's hide.

I loved to cook for other people, but cooking for others was actually part of my obsession with food. I felt virtuous in my ability to restrain from eating, and this boosted my self-esteem. My body was crying out "Feed me!" but I failed to respond.

The Effects of Starvation

An anorexic person in the throes of illness will never tell you this, but I can tell you from my own experience: living with anorexia on a daily basis is miserable. Worse than my depression or my obsessive thoughts and compulsions were the physical effects of my state of starvation.

I was always cold—so cold that my lips and fingernails stayed blue even in the summertime, even with several layers of clothing. The word "cold" takes on a new meaning when you're anorexic. It's a chilled-to-the-bone kind of cold. I have never been cold to the same extent since my recovery.

Starved of nutrients, my brain went haywire. All my waking moments were filled with disturbing thoughts. I was never insane or psychotic, but I often felt as if I were. (The key element in psychosis is the loss of touch with reality. In other words, had I believed that my thoughts and behavior were completely normal, then I would have been actually psychotic.)

Throughout my years of anorexia, I suffered from chronic depression. During times of depression, I lost interest in the things that had once brought me pleasure. Small everyday activities became a huge chore. I was always tired, even after sleeping for long periods. Getting myself out of bed became increasingly difficult. I often spent entire days in bed, in an attempt to escape the world. The world had lost all its color, and life had lost all its joy and meaning.

Starvation made my sleep not just fitful but nearly nonexistent. My body was on hyper alert most of the time. When I did manage to sleep, it was for only an hour or so. It was as if my body knew it was in crisis and had activated the fight-or-flight response. My mind was constantly racing with my obsessive thoughts, which made it all the harder to drift off. I was uncomfortable lying down because my protruding bones got sore when I lay on them. I was also cold. I tried an egg-crate mattress, but it didn't help much. Finally my mother bought me a heated waterbed, which did help, but I continued to get too little sleep.

The state of malnutrition caused some unusual physical changes, such as the loss of my menstrual cycle. And there was a more permanent effect, in that I've been diagnosed with osteoporosis. (In those who have had anorexia, osteoporosis persists after weight is regained and the menses return. After the age of 30, women can only retain—not gain—bone mass, and over time bone is lost as estrogen levels decline.) I'm told that I fall in the category of moderate fracture risk.

Also, once I had reached a certain state of malnutrition, my hair began to fall out. It's a good thing my hair is naturally thick. I never became bald, but I lost a lot of hair. Each morning, after my shower, there would be handfuls of hair on the bathroom floor. My hair became so thin that I'm sure some people wondered if I had cancer.

As I slowly starved, I developed other symptoms such as hyper-acute hearing. This was disturbing because it made it seem that people were yelling when they were only speaking in normal voices. I used to back away, or completely remove myself from places where people were talking, because the volume bothered me so much. My ears actually hurt or began to ring in response to normal sounds. This sensitivity to noise only furthered my isolation. As a compensatory mechanism, I spoke in a very soft voice, hardly above a whisper. My therapists probably thought I was just meek and insecure. I definitely was insecure, but that wasn't the reason for my hushed voice.

Then there was my thinking, which slowed dramatically. I often began a sentence and then lost track of my thought, so that I was unable to complete whatever I was saying. It seemed as if my thoughts were moving in slow motion. Things that were once very easy for me became difficult. I often read passages of material for school and then had no memory of what I had just read. At times, I felt as if I were going senile.

In summary, I felt bad all the time. Anorexia afflicts both the body and the mind. I was cold, tired, hungry, depressed, and plagued by obsessive thoughts. Fortunately, effective treatments do exist. After nearly six years of illness, I was in dire need of finding the one that would work for me.

8

A Faint Light at the End of the Tunnel

After years of searching for someone who would listen to me without preconceived notions, I met Dr. Jonathan Schultz, a soft-spoken older man with a receding hairline. Dr. Schultz came highly recommended and was said to have done extensive research on anorexia. He worked at a world-renowned medical center, to which my mother and I journeyed to meet him. At our first meeting, Dr. Schultz listened intently to what I had to say, never judging or criticizing me, from time to time jotting a note. For a brief while, I saw him as an outpatient, and I appreciated that he didn't just slap me in the hospital right away.

A Different Kind of Doctor

In addition to actually listening to me, Dr. Schultz did another thing that nobody before him had done: he asked me about my previous hospitalizations and what I thought had gone wrong with them. I couldn't believe that someone cared to know how my previous experiences had been for me. More importantly, I couldn't believe that this doctor didn't blame me for the previous treatment failures.

I told Dr. Schultz in great detail about my time at Presbyterian Hospital, and he was very understanding and supportive. He actually laughed when I told him about the pranks I had played on Dr. Bailey with my friend Melissa. He told me, "Your fighting spirit and sense of humor were the things that helped pull you through that experience."

Soon after I began seeing him, Dr. Schultz recommended hospitalization, promising that it would be unlike any of my previous confinements. My weight was down to sixty-five pounds, and I knew I needed help. My thinking was cloudy, I felt awful physically, and my obsessive thoughts were unabated. I willingly agreed to enter Saint Joseph's Hospital.

Coming to a Pivotal Point

When I was admitted to Four Northwest, little did I know that it would become my home for the next sixteen and a half months, or that my stay there would prove to be a pivotal point in my recovery. I was placed on the adolescent psychiatric unit with a whole variety of patients whose diagnoses ranged from adjustment disorders to depression. At the time of my admission, I was the only eating-disordered patient on the unit. That meant I didn't have to compete with anyone else to be the skinniest, nor did I have to worry about what tricks others were playing and whether they were getting away with more bad behavior than I was.

Saint Joseph's occupied a large, historic hospital building. A receptionist (I think she was a nun) guided my mother and me to the adolescent psychiatric unit, where a staff member answered the door and welcomed us inside.

We walked down a long, carpeted hallway. The color scheme appeared to be subdued blues. I was glad to see that the unit was missing the smoky haze I had grown accustomed to. Several staff members were playing Ping-Pong with the patients. It was a hopeful sign that they were actually out interacting, rather than secluding themselves behind glass in the nurses' station. Perhaps these people would have more understanding, more empathy for my predicament. Maybe they wouldn't blame me for the anorexia and punish me by taking my books away and making me stay in my room all day without use of the telephone.

I was escorted to the nurses' station and followed the admitting nurse to my room. There we went through the standard interview and history-taking process, and then I was allowed some time to unwind.

Shortly before the dinner hour, my mother was asked to leave, and I once again found myself alone in an unfamiliar environment. The unit guidelines and expectations had been described to me in brief by Dr. Schultz, so at least I had some idea what to expect.

Most of the kids ate in the large dining room, where food was served family style and everyone helped themselves. I was ushered into what was known as the small dining room, a secluded room where my tray came up, premeasured and calculated, from the dietary department. Starting that evening, a staff member sat one-on-one with me during each meal. The mealtime arrangement was the best I had experienced while in treatment, because I had direct staff support and supervision and didn't have to compete with fellow anorexics.

On the Eating Disorders Unit, I had spent a lot of time silently competing with the other patients. If someone at the dining room table got away with hiding food, I tried to get away with hiding even more food. If someone sneaked exercise, I tried to sneak even more exercise. It was like a game, but it became all-consuming. At least I didn't have that to contend with at St. Joseph's.

Off to a Rough Start

However, things didn't start off all that easily. The rule was that I was supposed to sit in front of my tray until I finished everything on it. I was started on a diet of only eight hundred calories per day, yet their expectations still seemed unreasonable to me. For the first several days, I sat with my trays all day, until bedtime, steadfastly refusing to eat. I continued to lose weight. Finally the doctors took over.

The treatment team consulted the metabolic support team, and I was placed on parenteral nutrition, or intravenous feedings. After the intravenous feedings were started, I was not required to go to meals or sit in front of my trays, and I spent nearly all my time in bed. I was very cold and weak, and sitting in chairs hurt me because I was so bony. I was grateful that I was no longer forced to sit in front of my trays for hours on end. It wouldn't have been of any therapeutic benefit, and Dr. Schultz knew that.

I was scheduled to have a Hickman catheter placed in the superior vena cava of my heart, but my mother once again refused to sign the surgery consent form. Shortly thereafter, a Dobhoff nasogastric tube was placed, and I was switched to tube feedings. Gradually, I gained weight. As my weight increased, I spent less time in bed and began to participate more in the daily program. Eventually, after my thought processes were a little clearer and I was physically stronger, I agreed with Dr. Schultz to begin eating. As I gradually increased my oral intake, my tube feedings were at the same time titrated down. It was a system that worked well.

The Psychodynamic Approach

Despite my early problems at Saint Joseph's, the staff remained caring, supportive, and nonjudgmental. Unlike the staff at Memorial, who had advocated a behavior-modification approach based on a system of rewards and punishments, the staff at Saint Joseph's had been trained to use a psychodynamic treatment approach. This method aims to resolve underlying emotional conflicts by using talk therapy to uncover unresolved childhood issues, while supporting a person through the recovery process.

The feeding methods employed were never administered in a punitive or degrading manner, which separated this experience from so many of my previous ones. I know that I really tried the staff's patience on numerous occasions, and yet they always remained professional. I came away knowing that even though the staff often disapproved of what I had done, they didn't dislike me as a person. They only disliked what I had done—an important distinction. I gradually gained enough trust to open up and talk to some of the nurses and doctors who were trying to help me.

A Well-Organized Program

The program at Saint Joseph's Hospital was unlike any of my previous hospitalizations, in several different ways. First, they were set up for long-term stays and had an organized school program right on the unit. I was the oldest person on the unit (nearly twenty-one at the time). An exception had been made to the standard rule—which allowed ages five to eighteen only—because Dr. Schultz worked solely out of this unit. There were four different teachers and classrooms. Each teacher taught at least two subjects, and the students rotated from classroom to classroom on a schedule. Theodore, one of the teachers, tutored me as I worked on my college correspondence courses. I managed to complete several classes that were eventually applied to my college degree.

In addition to the daily school program, each of us had a privilege level. On the highest level, green, you could actually go on short walks outside by yourself. (I never attained that privilege level.) The lowest level was red, which is where I remained for what seemed like forever. On the red level, you were basically confined to the unit. The blue privilege level was just above the red level. The blue level wasn't bad. As I recall, you could go bowling and take supervised walks.

Eventually, kids earned enough privileges to go on many different outings, including walks, picnics, movies, bowling, roller skating, and to the shopping mall. Besides weekends, outings were planned for several evenings each week. The regularly scheduled outings helped the routine seem more like ordinary daily life and less like institutional living. It established a sense of normalcy in our lives that I believe was one of the strong points of the program.

Dr. Schultz remained in charge of my care for the first three months of my stay, and I progressed fairly well. I was gradually weaned off the tube feedings and resumed responsibility for consuming my own daily requirements. I gained the privilege of filling out my own menus, with help from a supportive dietitian.

Physically, I was much stronger. The obsessive thoughts persisted, but they had lessened considerably from the time of my admission. Things were looking up.

In addition to my work with Dr. Schultz, I started working with Dr. Jean Hagen, one of the psychiatric residents. She was kind, empathetic, and nonjudgmental. I began to let down my guard and started doing some real psychotherapeutic work—talking about my early childhood experiences, Bobby, and my parents' divorce.

A Disruptive Change

Three months into my stay, the medical staff was abruptly rotated. Dr. Schultz was no longer the psychiatric head of the unit, and I wasn't allowed to see him anymore. I could tell that Dr. Schultz felt almost as bad about this change as I did, and he promised to stay informed of my progress. He assured me that I'd be able to see him again following my release from the hospital. Every now and then I caught a glimpse of him when he was passing by the unit. He used to try to give me encouragement, and I knew that he kept updated about my progress through interaction with my new doctors.

Not long after Dr. Schultz was rotated off our unit, he suffered a massive heart attack and had quadruple bypass surgery. I was told that he was asking about me from his bed in the critical care unit. To Dr. Schultz, I was more than a patient. I was a person. I was relieved to hear that he had recovered and returned to work.

At the same time that I lost Dr. Schultz, Dr. Hagen was also rotated, to be replaced by a new resident named Dr. Leah Collins. I felt really let down by the unexpected change of staff. After years of resistance, I had just begun to open up in therapy. Now I would have to start all over again from the beginning.

Dr. William Johnson was the new psychiatric head of the unit, and Dr. Collins worked under him. I had a hard time adjusting to the sudden change, and my loss of weight reflected that fact. Dr. Johnson's approach to running the unit was much different from that of Dr. Schultz. It was clear that they had different philosophies. The inconsistency in the treatment plan was difficult for me, with my rigid thinking. Drs. Johnson and Collins never bothered to sit down with me and ask me how I felt about losing the people with whom I had shared my deepest, darkest secrets.

Losing Ground

In the next three months, I lost much of the ground I had previously gained. My weight plummeted, and I engaged in another mental war against the medical personnel. Dr. Collins more than once told me, "You're going to wind up in a state mental hospital." Where had I heard that before? I recall wondering, *Why did she tell me that?* I felt that she purposefully said things to upset me.

Even though Saint Joseph's adhered to an enlightened psychodynamic treatment philosophy, the program had several big flaws. One was the inconsistency in the treatment efforts brought about by the frequent change of medical staff. By the time I had my program figured out, it would change again. During the later part of my hospitalization, after the abrupt change of staff, I was also allowed to lose weight and maintain a severely malnourished state. The message that was conveyed to me, through the staff's inaction, was that they didn't care about me. Once again, I was in my predicament alone.

As my weight dropped, my obsessions resumed control. I used to jog in my tiny closet, for hours on end. I jogged until my feet bled and I almost passed out from the heat. The staff became frustrated with trying to stop my exercising and rituals, and physically restrained me in the seclusion room. This increased my sense of loss of control over my life. Dr. Collins prescribed the antipsychotic medication Thorazine, previously used unsuccessfully on me by Dr. Nelson, to try to sedate me and control my behavior. When I refused to take it orally, I was given painful intramuscular injections that left me incapacitated for the entire day. I slept most of those days away in a drugged stupor.

Commitment

After the abrupt change of medical personnel, I decided to try to leave against medical advice. Shortly thereafter, commitment proceedings were brought. I felt angry at the staff for trying to keep me against my will, and decided to declare war against Dr. Collins.

For those of you who don't know, commitment proceedings are an ugly business. I was taken to the hearing by several deputies, who handcuffed me and drove me to the courthouse in a squad car like a criminal. It must have looked pretty pathetic to bystanders: several big deputies leading a young, emaciated woman into the courthouse in shackles. They didn't need the cuffs. Had I tried to get away, one of them could have just sat on me. Besides, I wasn't foolish enough to try to get away, nor did I have the energy.

Inside the courthouse, Dr. Collins sat on one side of the courtroom with my mother, while I sat on the other side with my county-appointed attorney. The proceedings didn't take long. Dr. Collins told the court all kinds of disparaging things about me, right to my face. She said all the standard things to get me committed: "She's a danger to herself," "She's mentally incompetent," and so on. Not all of the things were true, but it didn't matter because the judge believed her, of course. After sitting through that experience, I was supposed to go back to the unit and spill my private thoughts to this woman who sat glaring at me in the courtroom. Not on your life.

In any event, I was committed. I returned to the unit from the courthouse with a new cause. All of my energy was now directed toward freeing myself from the commitment. As soon as I could after the proceedings, I contacted my lawyer and requested an appeal. I ended up appealing the commitment three times over the next year and a half.

*　　*　　*

A Broken Toe and a Good Prank

Prior to the second appeal, I had an unpleasant exchange with Dr. Collins. She said something unkind and unprofessional that upset me. After she left the room, I was so angry at her that I kicked the cement wall, shattering the bones in my big toe. This incident happened immediately before my second court appearance. Although I was in great discomfort, I didn't tell anyone what had happened until after the hearing. I had to have three different surgeries to repair my toe. They ended up fusing the joint because it had been completely destroyed by the accident.

My friend Melissa and I still wrote to each other on a regular basis. She even came several times to visit me at Saint Joseph's. She had been released from the state hospital, and her weight was stable. One afternoon when Melissa came to visit, we were feeling mischievous as ever, so we devised a great caper specifically for Dr. Collins: we anonymously sent her my smelly old surgical shoe. Through the years, I hadn't lost my enjoyment of a good prank. Melissa and I got a good chuckle out of that one.

Amy Foster

Dr. Amy Foster, a slight young woman with blonde hair and an empathetic face, was one of the more caring psychiatric residents working on our unit. She wasn't assigned to my case, but she used to talk to me on occasion. When we talked, I got the feeling that she really understood my feelings and didn't judge me.

Dr. Foster worked in the clinic under the direction of Dr. Schultz. I almost had the sense that she had been where I now was, at some time in her life. We formed an immediate bond. During her three-month rotation on the adolescent psychiatric unit, I continued to see Dr. Foster during crisis intervention times when she happened to be on call. Looking back, I think I landed myself in the seclusion room a few extra times when I knew she was on call, just to have someone understanding to talk to. During that period, I felt that she was the only person in the world who understood me.

I continued my private war against Dr. Collins. I also continued in my daily maladaptive patterns, and no one on the unit tried to stop me. I didn't feel that I had much to live for. Outside the hospital, life went on for everyone else, while my life and my world remained static behind locked doors. Eventually, and to my great delight, Dr. Collins was rotated off the unit.

Unfortunately, Dr. Foster left at the same time. I was deeply saddened by her absence. She used to take me, in defiance of the rules, for brief walks outside the locked doors of Four Northwest, and I missed our little off-unit jaunts. Dr. Foster had added a caring human perspective to a world that often seemed cold, harsh, and uncaring.

Released at Last

Several other doctors, all of them more compassionate than Dr. Collins, tried to help me during my stay on the adolescent psychiatric unit. I just wasn't suited for therapy at that point. I'm sure my state of malnutrition contributed to that fact. Eventually, the staff gave up on my case. I was released and allowed to attend their day program on the same unit. The sixteen-month hospitalization had nearly exhausted my medical insurance funds, the inpatient program had little more to offer me, and the staff felt that I was stable enough to start a structured day program.

The additional freedom only made my condition worse. Each night I jogged the streets of the city, often using poor judgment in my choice of surroundings. Luckily nothing befell me, but it could have, since I ran by the train tracks at all hours of the night. I resumed therapy with Dr. Schultz, who remained supportive but was frustrated by my lack of progress.

My mother later told me that Dr. Schultz had said I exhibited one of the worst cases of anorexia nervosa he had ever seen. This statement was made by an international expert on the treatment of anorexia. I'm proud to say that I recovered, nevertheless.

On my third commitment appeal, I successfully bargained with the judge to be released to another treatment facility. Once transferred, I soon checked myself out against medical advice.

9

Partial Recovery

My return to health was not an instantaneous event; it happened over the course of several years. Several individuals played a part in my eventual full recovery. One was Dr. Jonathan Schultz. With his unconditional caring and support, he helped to break the wall of resistance I had created in response to the many failed treatment attempts.

Dr. Amy Foster also helped me, with her unending patience and faith in my ability to recover. Without her support, I wouldn't have made it. When I left Saint Joseph's Hospital, I had no idea that I would ever see her again. I certainly didn't know the continuing influence she would have in my life.

Not long after I was released from Saint Joseph's, Dr. Foster completed her residency, and I began seeing her as an outpatient. Dr. Schultz was not seeing patients due to his heart condition, so I'd been left without a psychiatrist. For the first time, I was the one making the choice about who I'd see as a therapist. I already knew that I got along with Dr. Foster. I respected her, although I didn't always like the things she made me do (like making me gain weight, or go into the hospital when I became physiologically unstable).

* * *

My Work With Dr. Foster

During the most acute phase of anorexia nervosa, the sufferer regresses to a childlike state. In that period of my life, I was very needy. I cried easily and was always anxious and afraid. I required continual reassurance. Dr. Foster, unlike any physician before or after her, was always there for me, twenty-four hours a day. I carried her pager number with me everywhere. Since I hardly slept, I called her at all hours. She always returned my calls promptly and would talk to me for as long as it took to calm me. I'm grateful for her extraordinary nurturing and support. I could never repay her for what she has done for me, but I will be forever thankful. I owe my life to her.

I wish I could say that all of the time spent with Dr. Foster was productive, but I spent many of my early sessions talking pointlessly about my rituals and obsessions. I used to tell Dr. Foster how much I hated myself when I gained weight. She just couldn't seem to grasp that concept; she was like my previous therapists in that respect. I would complain, "Look at me. I'm so fat! I just hate myself. I wish I could curl up and die!" Dr. Foster would reply, "Judy, you're delusional. Look at yourself. You're so thin." The time spent arguing about my weight could have been better used talking about the issues that were keeping me anorexic. But it was easier to avoid getting into what was really troubling me. In time, as my weight reached healthier levels, our sessions became more meaningful.

I was hospitalized several more times under Dr. Foster's care. Unfortunately, I can't tell you that I soared through the programs with ease. I was still what the staff members would consider a problem patient. The one thing that I did gain from the hospitalizations was a more healthy nutritional status, which provided the basis for more effective work in therapy. Dr. Foster required that I maintain a minimally acceptable weight. Although I wasn't fond of the idea, I trusted her and believed that she knew what she was talking about. Maintaining a minimal weight wasn't easy for me, but as I worked through some of my issues in therapy, it became less difficult.

My progress had its ups and downs. I would do better for a while, then get scared and regress. Gradually, the good days began to outnumber the bad. With Dr. Foster's gentle guidance, I was finally working through old "stuff." I had been out of commission for so long, and was still emotionally stuck where I'd been when my illness began. More meaningful therapy began when I started to work through some of the problems that had plagued me in early adolescence. Dr. Foster and I spent hours discussing my feelings of loneliness, the double standards in our family, my feelings of inadequacy about living up to my parents' expectations, the guilt surrounding my parents' divorce, and the loss of Bobby when I was only four. I gained much insight through this process.

Coming to Terms With My Parents' Divorce

I spent a lot of time resolving internal conflict regarding my parents' divorce. Only under Dr. Foster's care did I even start to work in this area. I was carrying a lot of inappropriate guilt over the divorce. It took a long time for the whole story to come out in therapy, because I was still so concerned with protecting my family—especially my mother. I spent hours recalling specific incidents from that time, while carefully watching Dr. Foster's responses. She never seemed shocked by what I told her and was continually supportive of me.

I told her how I used to find my mother crying in the middle of the night while everyone was sleeping. I confessed how I had secretly wished my parents would split, because I knew my mother wasn't happy. I recalled how desperately I wanted both of my parents to be happy, although that seemed so impossible.

I described my relationship with our houseguest, my father's research assistant—how he was at times more of a father to me than my own dad. Sometimes I wished that my mother would get a divorce and marry Brandon, and I felt guilty for that. I told Dr. Foster about my mother's feelings for this person who had come into our lives, and how she had asked me to "set the record straight" at the office when rumors were flying around the place my parents worked. Remembering how I circulated around my parents' office, zealously trying to clear my mother's reputation, I described how conflicted and guilty that had made me feel.

After my parents separated, my mother often spent weekends away. My sister and I knew she was going to see Brandon, but Mother always denied it. When I straight out said, "Mom, I know you're going to see Brandon," she replied, "No I'm not. Don't you tell me where I'm going, when you don't know. I'm just going away for the weekend, and that's it!" Her cover-ups confused me because they denied the validity of my perceptions. I told Dr. Foster how I'd worried about my father. Except for the time my brother had to leave, I'd never seen him so sad. I shared with her how I took on my mother's guilt when she openly showed her feelings for Brandon.

Through my work with Dr. Foster, I gradually came to understand that I wasn't responsible for what had happened. It wasn't until much later that I actually allowed myself to feel angry about the situation. I was still a child at the time of the divorce, and that experience aged me beyond my years. I still needed my mother to act as my parent. I shouldn't have had to be a parent to her.

Grieving for Bobby

I also worked through some issues relating to my brother's autism. I have always felt as if my twin is a part of me. There have been times when he was in difficulty at a great distance from me—hospitalized with seizures, perhaps—and somehow I've known. Bobby and I share a special bond, a second sense, an extraordinary gift that only twins can comprehend.

One time when we were eighteen I called the facility where he was staying in West Virginia and asked to speak to him. The person who answered said, "Bobby's been having trouble. He hasn't spoken to anyone in months. If you want, I can hold the phone to his ear, but he won't talk to you." I said, "That's okay. I just want to talk to him." Bobby came to the phone. I said, "Hello, Bobby. Do you know who this is?" "Dudy," he answered. "That's right," I said. "How are you?" He replied, "You doing fine." "Good," I said. "Do you know that your sister misses you?"

Bobby came back to live in a Minneapolis group home when we were twenty-one. His proximity to my mother's house made it easy for me to visit him. He knew when I was close to death and tried to comfort me as best he could, saying, "Don't cry." He perceived my pain and wanted to ease it.

During my sessions with Dr. Foster, I worked through my feelings regarding Bobby and his diagnosis. I finally came to terms with the fact that he will never get well, despite what my parents promised me as a child. I grieved his loss, going through all the stages of grief that one goes through: first denial, then anger and sadness. I finally arrived at acceptance. I have learned to love him for who he is, and I realize that whatever is was meant to be.

Sister Regina, the woman who became my godmother, would later tell me, "Your brother is one of God's children. He is so innocent. Bobby is able to appreciate all of the small things that everyone takes for granted. We could all stand to learn something from your brother." I found Sister Regina's insight comforting. She helped me to see Bobby in a whole new light—as a gift to our family, not a burden or a failure.

Facing My Feelings

I used my time in therapy with Dr. Foster to get in touch with feelings I'd been suppressing for most of my life. Starving myself or bingeing had been my way of effectively blocking out feelings. Emotionally, I was as numb as an alcoholic who passes out after one drink too many.

Dr. Foster asked me questions to try to get me to identify my feelings. Initially the process was very frustrating for me. I didn't know what I felt. I often responded to her questions by saying, "I just plain don't know what I feel."

What am I supposed to feel? What do you want me to say? I wondered. I watched her face for clues to the appropriate response. Sometimes my frustration with the process moved me to tears. "I can't do this. I'm a failure. See, I can't even get the therapy thing right," I told her. Dr. Foster remained patient, sometimes offering suggestions of possible feelings I might have had in a given situation. She would say something like, "Well, a lot of people in your situation would feel angry or sad or depressed. Did you experience any of those feelings?" Gradually, I learned to identify and name my feelings.

One thing I now learned was the importance of acknowledging anger—a taboo emotion in my family. As a child, I was told, "It's not okay to be angry. Go to your room." I wanted to please my parents, so I did my best to hide my unacceptable feelings. Later, I used to tell therapists that I never got angry, and I really believed it.

During my childhood, I got very good at disguising my emotions. I used to smile when I really wanted to run to my room and cry my eyes out. I was a very emotional child, and the stress of holding all my feelings inside made me feel like an emotional time bomb. After all those years of suppressing my feelings, it was hard for me to get back in touch with them. It was like learning a foreign language.

I now understand how the anorexia became a means of expressing the anger that my parents' rules forbade me to display. By not eating, I could take out my anger on myself and it was okay, because I wasn't hurting anyone else.

With Dr. Foster, I learned that feeling angry is okay. She told me, "It's what you *do* with your anger that can be either constructive or destructive." When I described certain situations to her, she would ask, "Does that make you angry?" My first response was always, "No, of course not." She often responded by saying, "Well, that would make a lot of people angry. You know that it's okay to feel angry." Her statements helped me take a second look, and often I would then realize that I had, in fact, been angry.

A People Pleaser

In addition to my difficulty identifying feelings, I spent my early years working so hard to please people that often I didn't know my own preferences. My mother has a strong personality and readily voices her opinions. I was her first healthy child, and a girl. My therapists have always thought it symbolic that my mother named me after herself, although she claims it was my father's idea. It sometimes seemed that she lived vicariously through me.

When people asked me questions, my mother often answered for me. That was always my father's pet peeve. I didn't mind it at the time, but looking back I can see that it undermined my self-esteem, sending the message that I couldn't possibly know my own mind. I used to agree with my mother's answers, so I never learned to be aware of my own thoughts. When we shopped for clothes and I showed my mother something, saying, "Mom, look. I like this," she sometimes replied, "That's ugly. You don't like that." I would then sheepishly put the item back. My mother still tends to do that today, but now I'm able to stand up to her and say, "You may not like it, but I do."

An Attempt at Normal Life

After my release from Saint Joseph's Hospital, I had the opportunity to start college. I chose a small, private Catholic women's college because I wanted the smaller classes and the more personal atmosphere. I moved into the freshman dorm and was paired with a nursing student named Christine. She and I attended many classes together, and became immediate friends.

I enjoyed my newfound freedom and the college lifestyle. School helped to give my life direction again. I explored the pros and cons of different majors, including music, biochemistry, and nursing. After several months, I was fairly sure that I wanted to major in biochemistry and go on to medical school. I met a wonderful chemistry professor, Sister Martha, who inspired and encouraged me.

I became active in the college orchestra and started to study violin under a member of a well-known professional orchestra. I was even awarded a scholarship, which paid for my music lessons. Life was beginning to look brighter.

Unfortunately, even though other parts of my life were going well, my eating disorder didn't disappear. The freedom of living on campus gave me unrestrained liberty in my eating and exercise behavior, and I wasn't yet ready for that. My weight plummeted.

I needed to take a course in nutrition for my major. On the first day, before the class had gotten under way, the professor singled me out and publicly told me that I couldn't attend her class. I was extremely embarrassed. I didn't understand why I was being asked to leave. The professor said, "You obviously don't need this class," and refused to proceed with the lecture until I had removed myself from the room. I broke down in tears, and left the classroom in shame.

The experience shook my self-esteem. Eventually I was asked by the administration to leave school. I was told that the college didn't want to be responsible if I died on campus. (Liability, you know.) After being kicked out of college, I returned to the hospital until my weight was restored.

Although my first try at a college education had been unsuccessful, I now had a renewed purpose in life and a new goal to work toward. I was no longer in treatment merely to get better so that I could stay out of hospitals and institutions. I was in treatment so that I could finish college and make something of my life.

Suicide Attempts

I continued seeing Dr. Foster for several years, while my condition went up and down. I became discouraged and severely depressed. I still didn't want to die, but I felt that I couldn't continue living as I had been. The depression and hopelessness eventually led me to several suicide attempts.

The first attempt occurred in the fall of 1992. I had hit the depths of despair, and saw no way out my misery. My mother, fearing that I was too depressed to have it in my possession, had confiscated my car. In a determined effort to kill myself, I walked three miles to a local store and bought a large bottle of Extra-Strength Tylenol and a can of Diet Pepsi. I took the entire bottle of pills, gagging as I choked them down. Then I headed back home to my room to lie on my waterbed.

I lay there waiting for a bright light to appear and for my life to end. Suddenly I thought, *Oh no. What have I just done? What if God is mad at me for this? What if I go to Hell? I've got to tell someone.* I went downstairs and told my mother what I had done. In shock and tears, she telephoned the local ambulance. As the neighbors watched from their front porches, the paramedics loaded me into a bright red ambulance and carted me off.

I arrived in the emergency room to find a team of really fed-up nurses who scolded me, saying, "Look what you've just done. We have patients here who are truly sick—and then *you* come rolling in." An older, heavyset nurse then proceeded to shove a huge tube down my throat and pump my stomach to rid my body of the overdose. If I thought that was bad, the next step was worse.

Another woman in blue scrubs appeared, telling me, "Here. Drink this." It was a glass of charcoal to neutralize the Tylenol. The stuff looked like coal. It was thick, with big chunks. They had added sweetener to try to make it more palatable. I took a sip and gagged. "You're not serious. Really, you've got to be kidding. I'm supposed to drink this?" "Yes," she impatiently replied. When I refused, they put the tube back down my throat and poured the mixture into my stomach that way. An incredible wave of nausea passed over me.

"I think I'm going to be sick," I moaned. Explosively, I vomited the black charcoal mixture all over myself and the two nurses who were standing nearby. Then there was a whirlwind of activity. One nurse put in an IV while another one drew my blood. Somebody put patches on my chest and somebody else put a tube in my bladder. I was whisked upstairs to the intensive care unit, a place filled with bright lights, beeping machines, and scary-looking equipment. I had landed myself in an ICU on more than one occasion, and this time, too, I made it out alive.

The second attempt came only weeks after the first one. I overdosed on twice as much Extra-Strength Tylenol. I was quietly waiting for the drug to take effect when the toxic level of the Tylenol caused me to vomit violently, splattering my mom's beautiful white carpet. My mother was very concerned. I told her, "Don't worry, Mom. I probably just have a bad case of the flu. I'll feel better tomorrow." Thank goodness she didn't believe me. When I got to the emergency room, my drug level was very high. They told my parents that I might not make it, and that if I did, I'd probably need both a kidney and a liver transplant.

My sister flew out and stayed at my bedside twenty-four hours a day. My father, a captive of his work and still in denial about my illness, was unwilling to fly out to see me. Anne spent the days curled up on the foot on my bed reading to me, while monitors beeped in the background. I faded in and out of consciousness. One afternoon she turned to me and said, "Judy, you can't die. What would I do without you?"

My Spiritual Awakening

Each morning my blood was assessed for kidney and liver damage. Every day for the first two weeks, the levels were progressively worse. I had never been religious, but I started praying anyway. Miraculously, I made it through with no residual liver or kidney damage.

The doctors were astounded when my blood tests showed a complete reversal of the damage. I believe it was an act of God; there is no other explanation. That experience was the beginning of my spiritual awakening. I thought to myself, God must have some higher plan or purpose for my life. I began to pray daily for the strength, guidance, and courage to overcome my eating disorder.

Shock Treatments

Following my release from the ICU, I was admitted to the psychiatric unit. The psychiatrist in charge of my care suggested electroconvulsive therapy (ECT). I resisted what I considered to be a barbaric treatment modality, but eventually the professionals won out. I ended up having fifteen individual ECT treatments—two and a half times the standard number.

On the morning of my first treatment, a cheerful nurse entered my room and said, "This is it. The doctors are ready. I need you to go to the bathroom and then put on this gown." She fastened a name band around my wrist and loaded me onto a stretcher. I was wheeled down a long hallway and through a set of green metal doors into the dreaded room, where an anesthesiologist was waiting for me. My head got woozy, and then I was out. I awoke in my room with an incredible headache, and slept the rest of the day away.

I was told that the ECT treatments might produce a temporary memory loss, but that I would eventually regain my memories. To this day, I have not regained them. My memory loss was disturbing. I returned to school and couldn't recall attending classes or even taking notes that were written in my own writing. People used to walk up to me and say, "Hi, Judy." I'd greet them in return, pretending I knew who they were when, as far as I knew, I'd never seen them before in my life. The experience was quite disorienting.

Susan

When I recovered from the near-fatal overdose, my mother's therapist suggested that I try a new therapist. Bob was my mother's therapist; I had seen him, on occasion, for family sessions. He was concerned that my therapy with Dr. Foster had reached a standstill, and told my mother about another female therapist whom he highly recommended. When my mother presented the idea to me,

I resisted at first. I had formed a relationship with Dr. Foster and wasn't eager to work with anyone else. Yet I agreed to meet the woman Bob had suggested. We agreed that it would be my decision whether I continued with her as a therapist.

On the way to my first meeting with Susan, I parked my Honda in the lot and rode a glass elevator to the top floor of an old, renovated school building. I walked into a cozy little office with a big skylight and settled myself on a couch with plump pillows. Susan was a tall, attractive, middle-aged blonde. I was impressed by her quiet manner. She laid down the ground rules from day one, telling me that she would not talk to my mother unless I was present and I consented to her doing so.

At first I didn't know what to think. All my previous therapists had talked to my mother behind my back to find out "how I was really doing." I knew that my mother would be upset if Susan wouldn't talk to her, so I said, "That's okay, you can talk to my mother. I don't care." Susan reiterated her statement. She told me that she was *my* therapist, pointing out that my mother had her own therapist. Looking back, I realize that the ground rules Susan laid down were the prerequisites to a true therapeutic relationship, one based on mutual respect and understanding.

Susan insisted that I call her by her first name. I wasn't used to this, but it was symbolic of the type of mutual relationship or partnership that would be built between us. The very word "Doctor" creates the feeling of a power discrepancy between therapist and client. Many people elevate a doctor to the level of some sort of supreme being, as in the old saying "The doctor knows best." Being on a first-name basis with Susan helped to level the playing field. Susan consistently demonstrated, through both her words and her actions, that we were equal participants in the therapeutic process.

10

Full Recovery

My sessions with Susan were different from most of my previous therapy in several important ways. One of these was that she somehow managed to steer the conversation away from my weight, my rituals and obsessions, and food. I think I knew that she wouldn't tolerate trivial talk. In the beginning, I used to tell her how distressed I was about my weight. She would listen very quietly to what I had to say. When I had finished, she would redirect the conversation by saying something like, "You look anxious today. Can you tell me about your week? Did something happen this week that made you upset?" Usually something *had* happened, and our talk was then steered into a productive area.

Susan's System

Unlike all of my previous therapists, Susan never argued with me about my weight and never tried to convince me I wasn't fat. She refused to enter into a power struggle with me over weight and eating. This was a wise decision on her part, because I've always been very stubborn and she never could have won. Susan hardly ever spoke about my weight. When she did mention it, her words were brief and her manner calm. I remember a time prior to my last hospitalization when she commented, "You've lost weight. Did you have a hard week? Do you want to tell me about it?"

Included in the initial ground rules laid down by Susan was the provision that Dr. Foster would take over my care if my weight fell below a certain level. During periods of hospitalization, I would not be able to see or speak with Susan. My sessions with her would resume after my release from the hospital. I'm sure that she laid down this provision to avoid the triangling that can occur when more than one therapist or healthcare professional is involved in a person's care. By the term "triangling," I mean the confused pattern of interaction that may occur when two different healthcare providers have conflicting goals or expectations for the anorexic individual and she is able to identify the differences and play them off against one another.

Susan's system worked well. During my nearly three years of therapy with her, I was hospitalized only once. That one hospital stay proved to be my very last hospitalization for anorexia.

My mother later told me she wished we had found Susan earlier. She thought I could have been spared some of the misery. That might have been the case, but I'm not sure. Susan was a great therapist for me; we were a good therapeutic match. Yet I don't know whether the outcome would have been the same if I had met her early in my illness.

Several factors favorably influenced my recovery process. First, I had really hit rock bottom. I knew I couldn't continue as I had been living. My worst fear—placement in a state mental hospital—was not far from materializing. I wasn't about to let that happen. Next, my weight had stabilized in a range where my thoughts were more clear, and this enabled me to really work in therapy. Finally, I'd had the opportunity to experience some moments of freedom while away at college. I knew that I wanted to complete college, and this became a new goal to work toward.

I saw Susan weekly, and through the weeks and months and years told her the intimate details of my childhood and early adolescence, of my previous treatment experiences, of my current daily life. Susan listened carefully to my stories and provided helpful feedback. She helped me learn to have faith in myself and my instincts. She repeatedly assured me that I wasn't crazy, but that some of the situations I had been placed in were crazy. She reiterated over and over again that I should have faith in my gut feeling or basic instinct, because it would always be correct. I doubted her at first, but gradually I came to believe in myself.

Watching the numbers go down on the scale had given me a temporary feeling of power. Susan was the first person to help me find other ways to gain a sense of control over my life. She helped me to channel my energy into productive areas. When I came into a session complaining that some area of my life was miserable and I was helpless to do anything about it, Susan would say, "Let's look at that a little further. Of course there are things you can do about it. Let's take a look and see what some of your options are." For the first time in years, I was reclaiming my own power. I was not helpless, nor was life hopeless and out of control. As I learned to take charge of some of the areas of my life that had felt out of control, both the anorexia and the obsessive-compulsive tendencies lessened.

I resumed college classes shortly after starting therapy with Susan. I thought long and hard about whether I wanted to go back to the same college, after being previously asked to leave the campus. One voice inside my head told me that I should go to a different school where nobody would know anything about me. I knew that it would be easier on my pride to go to a different school. But I also knew that the college I had attended previously was rated very highly in the area I wanted to major in. I didn't want to hang my head in shame and let my past dictate my future. I decided to meet the challenge head on and returned to the campus where I had studied before.

A Hindrance Named Ronald

Once I went back to school, I experimented with a variety of living situations. For a while, I lived on campus in the dorms. Next, I tried living at home with my mother and her current boyfriend. Ronald was unemployed and living the good life off Mom's income. And that wasn't the worst part about him. Ronald was what my mother called "not too stable." That was her delicate way of saying, "The guy is just plain nuts."

Ronald was an emotionally traumatized Vietnam veteran, and apparently that was what made him crazy. You never knew what would set him off. If you looked at him the wrong way or were wearing the wrong color of socks, that could be enough.

One time Ronald made a derogatory comment about my sweater, a special one that my mother had made for me. I blurted back, "It does not look homemade, it looks like someone put a lot of love and effort into it." Ronald was furious that I had dared to talk back to him. We were on our way to dinner at a posh restaurant. Once we got there, Ronald made a scene, ranting and raving at my mother that she hadn't raised me right. I felt embarrassed because all the people in the restaurant were staring at us.

Ronald had a hot temper and often lost control. One afternoon I returned home to find that, in a fit of rage, he had thrown a telephone through a wall. The room, littered with broken bits of my mother's favorite memorabilia, was in a shambles.

The worst part about Ronald was that I never felt safe around him. The instability I felt because of his presence in my life was the primary factor leading to my last hospitalization for anorexia. Over the two years that my mother was with him, things got so bad that I was afraid I would go home some time and find my mother dead. I realized just how bad the situation was when I found my mother sharpening kitchen knives. When I asked her what she was doing, she replied, "You never know when you might need them." Eventually, my mother wised up and terminated her relationship with Ronald.

My Final Hospitalization

My last hospitalization happened early in the course of my treatment with Susan. It was brief, lasting less than a month. I went in because I once again felt I'd lost control over my life, due to my having to live in the same house with a madman.

When I was ready to be released, Susan came to my discharge planning sessions to help coordinate an effective outpatient plan. I decided that I didn't want to go back home and chose to stay at a group home instead. I found the group-home living arrangement depressing because I was the only normal one there. The home was for young adults with chronic mental illness, so most of the residents floated in and out of psychosis. I spent most of my time watching television or talking with the college-aged staff. Imperfect though it was, the group-home option was preferable to returning to the chaos at home.

During one of our sessions, Susan asked me if I had ever thought of getting my own place. I just laughed at her and said, "Of course not." She pursued the issue, asking, "Why not?" I went into all the reasons why I couldn't do it and why it wouldn't work. After some discussion, Susan convinced me otherwise. Not long thereafter, I went looking for my own apartment.

I ended up finding a place in a wonderful old building near the college campus. My apartment had French windows, old woodwork, and high ceilings. I was excited to finally have a place of my own to call home.

For many years, my frequent hospitalizations had made the pursuit of a college education nearly impossible. Following my final hospital release, I enrolled in college courses once again. I was going to make a third try at obtaining a college degree. My boundless energy, of which a large portion had once been channeled into attaining the perfect thinness, was now fully directed toward completing my education.

My weight stabilized and remained stable, and I was able to focus on school. I excelled in my courses, making the dean's list my first semester. For the first time in my life, I was getting good grades just for myself. I no longer felt that I needed to win my parents' approval. More important than my scholastic excellence was the fact that, for the first time in nearly ten years, I was gaining satisfaction from something other than losing weight.

In addition to my required classes, I got involved in an extracurricular activity by joining the college orchestra. I had always derived a lot of pleasure from playing my violin, an outlet that had been left by the wayside during the depths of my illness. While a sophomore, I became the concertmaster of the college orchestra.

Embracing Catholicism

Around that time, I began to explore the idea of converting to Catholicism. I started attending St. Paul's Outreach, the youth group affiliated with my college. Almost immediately I felt a kinship, a sense of connection, an inner awakening. I was destined to become a Catholic. Sandy, one of my friends from the group, introduced me to Sister Regina, the woman who would later become my godmother. I took it a step further, attending a weekly informational meeting at the nearby Catholic men's college affiliated with my school. Finally, I made my decision and attended a year's worth of catechism classes at the local Catholic church. Sister Regina was my mentor.

Prior to my baptism, I attended a retreat at which I went to the priest and asked for forgiveness. I told him of my suicide attempts and the years of lies to my family to cover up my eating disorder. I felt God's presence in the room with me that day. A wave of relief washed over me; I knew I had been forgiven. I asked the priest, "Why have I had to suffer so? What is God's plan for me?"

He told me, "I can't answer that question for you. That is something *you* must find. Pray to God and ask Him for the answer. I will tell you this: God only gives people that which they can handle. He must have thought you were strong. You have the ability to take your knowledge and share it among others. I know that you will do good things."

I reflect on those words almost daily, and they always give me strength.

In a beautiful candlelight ceremony on Easter Sunday, I was baptized into the Catholic Church. On the day of the baptism, I was sick with the flu. I had invited a few close friends to attend the ceremony, and afterwards we went out to celebrate over cake and coffee. Then I went home to bed.

New Friends

On the personal front, I started to develop friendships. I had almost forgotten what it was like to have friends who weren't eating-disordered. During the years I spent locked up as a psychiatric patient, I didn't have a lot of good choices for my social life, so I kept to myself. Also, anorexia, by its very nature, is extremely isolating.

Prior to my illness, I had been self-conscious and uncomfortable in social situations. I had often felt that I didn't measure up to other people, and I worried that others were thinking bad things about me. When I entered a room full of strangers, I thought, *I wonder if they're looking at my Prednisone cheeks. I bet they think I'm fat. I hope they don't think I'm bookish and a nerd.*

Now I was learning that my old fears had been unfounded, and I was able to develop some lasting friendships.

I met Angie in a psychology class. She was a Catholic girl from a Polish family, with an incredibly warm smile and empathetic manner. We often talked after class. I learned that Angie suffered from obsessive-compulsive disorder, a psychiatric problem with symptoms similar to my own strange rituals and obsessions. I felt an immediate kinship with Angie. Maybe I wasn't alone in my struggle. Perhaps other people struggled, too—just less visibly.

I even started dating. Allen and I started seeing each other in the spring of 1992. He was six years older than I and worked for a transportation company as a dispatcher. We were an unlikely match, but somehow we hit it off. Allen had a great sense of humor. I have many fond memories of walks in the park, rides at the state fair, roasting marshmallows over an open campfire, evenings spent curled up under a blanket watching movies, and many trips to the local zoo. Allen was a kid at heart and had amassed a large collection of stuffed monkeys, starting when he was in the Marines and stationed overseas. My knowing him added a new dimension to my life.

I had been out of the mainstream for so long that I needed to relearn how to interact with people. And, of course, I didn't have a lot of previous social skills to fall back on. It was like learning to ride a bicycle for the first time—scary but also exciting. Gradually, I became more comfortable in social settings. I made a lot of good friends and made up for lost time. I learned that true friends like me for who I am. I don't have to create a facade—something I hated during high school. Finally I learned how to relax and have fun.

One of my friends, Colleen, was quite a comedian. She kept me laughing for hours on end. For the first time in years, I was laughing at something other than pulling the wool over some mental-health worker's eyes.

Reconnecting With Bobby

When I had some spare time, I would pick up Bobby at his Minneapolis group home to take him out for his favorite treat, a meal at Burger King. Then I'd take him for a ride in "Dudy's brown car" to my apartment. At stoplights, he would look at me and say, "The light will turn green." His innocence and pure heart delighted me and made me laugh.

Once we arrived at my apartment, I had to be careful that my school assignments didn't disappear. Bobby, wanting to be like me, often stuffed items from around the apartment into his backpack. Usually I set him up with crayons and paper to keep him occupied. He loved coloring space shuttles, and often left me with a nice new drawing for my refrigerator.

When it was time to take him back, Bobby would say, "Not going back to the group home."

"What about work?" I'd ask. "You have to go to work tomorrow."

"Not going to go to work. Going to sleep at Dudy's house," he'd answer.

Bobby truly blesses my life. He reminds me to appreciate the small things that are so easily taken for granted.

Melissa, My Fellow Survivor

While I was relearning the ropes of normal life, I stayed in close contact with my old partner in crime. Melissa was now married, and she and her husband had just bought their first home in a neighboring suburb. She had one child in hand and another on the way. Melissa worked night shifts at a security company, which made it hard for us to get together. Yet we still managed to spend hours on the phone, sharing the details of our daily lives.

Through the years, Melissa and I have maintained a holiday tradition in honor of our old nemesis, Dr. Bailey. We found a delightful Snoopy Christmas card, and purchased a box of ten. The greeting reads: "Dashing through the snow with a holiday hello." Each year for the past nine years, Melissa and I have sent Dr. Bailey the same card. Usually we also send a can of Ensure or a photo, or something else to jog his memory. We'd just hate to have him forget us.

I attended the birth of Melissa's first baby—a miracle child, since Dr. Bailey had told Melissa years earlier that she would never be able to bear children. The most recent holiday card to Dr. Bailey contained a picture of the two of us with Melissa's new baby and second child, Ericka. The card ritual has provided a sense of closure regarding that chapter of our lives.

Going Cold Turkey

During my early work with Susan, I continued seeing Dr. Foster for adjustments of my medication. I took an antipsychotic to help lessen my obsessions and compulsions, and also an antidepressant. I'd been told that, because I had a chemical imbalance, I would need to be on lifelong medication to regulate my moods. Yet, after less than a year in therapy with Susan, I felt prepared to go off all medication.

I knew that Dr. Foster and my mother wouldn't approve of my stopping the medication, and I wasn't sure that Susan would like it either. So I went cold turkey, informing the members of my care team only after the fact. To my relief, I didn't suffer any repercussions from the abrupt cessation of the chemicals. I continued to do well on an outpatient basis. I had always hated the way psychiatrists pushed pills on me, as if medication were the solution to my problem. Now I was living in a more natural state, without any artificial support. I felt newly empowered.

As I worked with Susan, the depression that had permeated my being for so many years finally lifted. The world around me had color once again, and my life had renewed purpose. I began to see the glass as half full rather than half empty. For every negative, there is a positive. I learned to seek, find, and appreciate the many positives. I learned that life offers us many choices. Being able to find and appreciate the many joyful aspects in my life helped the depression to dissipate and finally disappear. I learned that my thoughts influenced my feelings. If I told myself, *Life is horrible. I don't have any control over this situation, and it'll never get better,* I felt depressed. But if I told myself, *I don't like this situation. However, I do have choices. I'll pick the best choice, and I know things will get better,* I ended up feeling okay. By learning to change my negative thoughts, I increased my optimism. I was once again able to see the sunshine.

The other areas of my life continued to improve. I made it through one semester without hospitalization, then one semester turned into several. Before I knew it, I was halfway to obtaining my baccalaureate degree.

The restoration of a more normal body weight was one of the later things in my sequence of events. I'm grateful that Susan didn't push the weight issue. She required me to maintain a minimum weight—one conducive to effective psychotherapy—but beyond that, what I did with my weight was left up to me. Little by little, as my life began to feel more manageable, my weight climbed to a more normal level.

Several benefits reinforced the weight gain. First, people responded to me better. I no longer got the shocked and disapproving looks I used to get from strangers. Second, my thoughts were much clearer and I had more energy. Finally, I just felt better. I wasn't cold all the time. I could actually sleep at night. It didn't hurt to sit on a chair anymore.

Even after the restoration of my normal body weight, my uneasiness pertaining to food and eating continued. It took me several more years to completely eliminate my strange anorexic fears. For example, I considered certain foods taboo. I had coined the term "danger foods" to describe them. The thought of eating one of my danger foods provoked severe anxiety; I was afraid something bad would happen to me. I knew the thought was irrational, but was convinced that I'd gain an inordinate amount of weight by eating a single bite of something forbidden.

Susan was helping me to see how I used the anorexia to maintain a sense of control over my life. In order to free myself from my anorexic obsessions, I needed to find new ways to gain a sense of control. I sought out more positive ways to take charge of my life. As other areas of my life blossomed, my food fears diminished, and so did the related obsessions and compulsions.

Eventually Susan thought I was ready for group therapy. I started attending a weekly women's support group. This was not an eating-disorders group, which made it different from my earlier groups. I was the only one in the group who had suffered from an eating disorder, so I wasn't sidetracked by my competitive desire to be thinner than the other group members, or diverted by trying to fix others' problematic eating behaviors. (That competitive drive remained for several years after the restoration of my healthier body weight.)

The group therapy proved very helpful. In our weekly sessions, I was able to verify my perceptions about things going on in my life—family and early-childhood issues—with the other group members. It was through the group therapy sessions that I really learned to feel my feelings without guilt. During our meetings, I described family situations and my resulting feelings, and fellow group members gave me feedback. I realized that my feelings of anger or sadness didn't make me a bad person. Others in my group validated my feelings by suggesting that they would have felt the same way. I wasn't insane after all. Looking back, I believe that the group therapy really solidified my earlier work in individual therapy.

Making Peace With Dad

During the time I attended the women's group, I kept on seeing Susan, although less often, and continued to work through my issues. I even had a couple of family sessions with my father. With Susan's help, I learned to communicate more openly with Dad. I had always believed that my father blamed me for certain things that happened at the time of the divorce, and I'd avoided him because of this. I was finally able to ask him if this were, in fact, true. His answer allayed some of my fears. When I suggested that I was responsible for what had happened, my father actually laughed.

I also had a chance to tell him what it was like feeling that I could never live up to his expectations. As a child, I so badly wanted my father to say that he was proud of me. But he's a man of few words. Consequently, I didn't get the verbal reinforcement that I would have liked.

I don't blame my father, because I know that I pressured myself. From the time I was small, I looked at the accomplishments of my father and felt that I must live up to them. This was the man who had completed his undergraduate degree at Berkeley with a straight 4.0 GPA—one of twelve students in the history of the school to take the university medal. This was the well-respected man who will probably one day win the Nobel Prize for his contribution to the field of economics. How could I ever measure up?

In addition, I'm sure that I felt extra pressure to make up for what my twin brother couldn't do. Also, if I were found to be defective or couldn't measure up, would I be sent away like Bobby? Through my discussions with my father, I learned that he was proud of my accomplishments, and just assumed that I knew. Dad told me, "I'm really surprised to hear that you feel that way. Of *course* I'm proud of you. I thought you knew that. I'm sorry if I didn't acknowledge your accomplishments."

Further Benefits of Therapy

My sessions with Susan helped me to see certain situations in a more balanced way. As my self-esteem improved, I didn't internalize things as I used to do. My craving for positive feedback from others was replaced by an inner belief that my actions and accomplishments were valuable. I no longer needed other people to tell me I was worthwhile.

I continued to work on becoming more independent and differentiating myself from my mother. Having my own apartment helped a lot. The summer before my junior year in college, I expanded my independence by becoming more self-sufficient financially. I obtained a full-time position as a nurse's aide at a nursing home. I knew that the work wouldn't be easy, but some friends who were ahead of me in the nursing program had recommended it. They said that prior work as a nurse's aide would improve my chances of getting an internship in nursing between my junior and senior years, so I took my friends' advice.

In addition to the work on issues pertaining to my parents, I worked with Susan to gain a better understanding of my relationship with my sister. As a child, I had always believed we were polar opposites. Of course, we also had the typical sibling rivalry. Through therapy, I gained the realization that, although Anne and I showed our feelings differently, we had both gone through many of the same experiences. We were both affected by our early childhood. Neither of us had an easy adolescence, but I think Anne had a smoother time because she used to blow up and let her feelings out. Beneath our very different exteriors, we were feeling many of the same things. As adults, we have become good friends. Talking with Anne gives me insight into my own behavior.

Before starting my junior year in college, I completed my therapy with Susan. I walked away from our sessions feeling like a new person, with a new outlook on life. I can't describe how wonderful it felt to finally be free of the obsessions that had plagued me. Sometimes when I'm stressed, my obsessive-compulsive tendencies still flare, but they're not overwhelming the way they used to be and I'm able to stop myself from acting on them. Usually they manifest in benign behaviors such as repeatedly checking numbers in my checkbook. When I notice what I'm doing, I'm able to decide, *This is silly. I'll come back to it later.* I'm happy to say that I no longer have any strange food hang-ups.

Susan and I both cried at our last session, looking back on how far I'd come. I said my final good-bye, and then was set free to tackle life's challenges on my own.

I learned many important things from Susan, but several stand out in my mind. I learned that I could gain a sense of mastery over my life through means other than the anorexia. I also learned to differentiate the things that I could influence, such as my own actions and behavior, and the things that were out of my hands, such as other people's actions and behavior, my family, and my brother's autism. I spent many years trying to fix things that were beyond my power to fix, feeling helpless and frustrated when my efforts didn't succeed. I learned to let go of the things I couldn't change and focus on the things I could.

I came to recognize the fact that my self-worth as a person lies deep within me. It's not on the surface, and it can't be measured by reading a number off the bathroom scale. I learned to channel my energy in positive directions, toward things that would give me the satisfaction anorexia never could. I discovered a whole variety of truly pleasurable activities in which to partake.

The meaning and direction had been restored to my life. For the first time in years, I was happy in the real sense of the word.

11

Freedom

My junior year in college was the beginning of a new chapter in my life. For the first time in nearly ten years, I was completely free to live independently. I no longer had my weekly therapy sessions to fall back on for moral support, yet I felt well prepared to tackle the challenges that lay ahead.

Nursing School

The core curriculum in the baccalaureate nursing program starts in the junior year. Prior to that year, most of the course work is either a prerequisite or a basic liberal arts requirement. I well remember the first day of nursing class. We assembled in the large auditorium that was to be our base of operations for the next two years. All the nursing lectures were held in this auditorium. One hundred and eight students were present on that first day. Not surprisingly for a Catholic women's college, all but two were female. Some knew each other, but for the most part we were complete strangers. Many of the students had transferred here from a larger state school. We began to socialize, and started new friendships that would deepen during the course of the nursing program.

Academically, the program was demanding. We needed to do a lot of reading in order to write our many papers, and the preparation for our clinical practice days also took time. In the past, school had been easy for me. I had been able to study at the last minute and still get straight A's. Now that school had become more time-consuming, I decided to cut back my hours at the nursing home.

Unfortunately, the management where I worked didn't respect my change in hours very well. They often called me to say, "We need you to come in. We have X many residents and so-and-so called in sick." I tried telling them that I wasn't scheduled to work, but at times they almost demanded that I come in. I decided to find work elsewhere.

I ended up taking a position as a teaching assistant in the biology department at school. The pay was less than at the nursing home, but the stress was considerably less as well. I enjoyed my role as a teaching assistant and continued in the position until my graduation. As a TA, I was a mentor to other students. I was no longer the scrawny little anorexic, curled up in fetal position and tucked away in an institution somewhere. I was actually contributing to the education of other college students, and in that way giving something back to society.

I increased the range of my extracurricular activities by joining the Student Nurses Association. That year, I was elected to represent my state in the House of Representatives at the annual National Student Nurses Association Convention. I felt proud to be able to represent both my school and our state. It was a wonderful experience. In addition, I started participating in the Nurses Christian Fellowship group. Through my involvement in these and other activities, I met a lot of people and made many new friends.

The nursing curriculum made regular attendance at orchestra rehearsals impossible. Another student took my place as concert-master, and I continued to participate on an informal basis, attending rehearsals and concerts as my schedule permitted.

Allen and I grew apart. Things in my life were looking up at the same time that his life was starting to fall apart around him. Allen lost his job in early November and fell into a serious depression. I tried to be supportive, but I was frustrated by his lack of motivation to find another job. The more I pushed the issue, the worse our relationship became. Sometimes I had the sense that he was jealous of my accomplishments. I could see that our relationship would never work, and I broke up with Allen in December.

An Internship in Wisconsin

In November and December of my junior year, I began looking for an internship. Even before I started into the nursing curriculum, I had known that I wanted to work in an acute-care hospital setting. But the job opportunities for new graduate nurses were few, because the healthcare sector was in the midst of major cutbacks. I'd been told that my best chance for attaining an acute-care position was to secure an internship and continue working through my senior year at the same institution.

I sent out numerous letters of inquiry to large institutions, feeling discouraged by the lack of opportunities. Many big hospitals with previous long-standing internship programs weren't doing programs this year for lack of funds. I could understand their rationale; it would be hard to justify hiring interns for the summer when they were in the process of laying off long-term employees. I filled out the two application forms that I had received, crossed my fingers, and waited.

The deadline for hearing back from the two hospitals I'd applied to came and went. I was disappointed, but not devastated. I started to make alternative plans for summer employment, deciding that I'd try to find work as a nurse's aide in a local hospital to help get my foot in the door. I also took a position as a student nurse volunteer at a small local hospital. I did my volunteering on a unit where the patients' conditions were fairly acute. As a student nurse volunteer, I was allowed to do the things that a nurse's aide would do, only I didn't get paid for the job. I didn't mind the lack of pay, because I was gaining valuable experience.

One morning in February, I opened my mailbox to find a large, thick envelope from one of the hospitals I had applied to in early November. I was eager to open it, but decided not to do so in the stairwell of my building. Returning to my apartment, I held the envelope for several minutes, doing some "self-talk" so I wouldn't be too disappointed when I discovered I'd been turned down. I told myself they'd probably just mailed all my application materials back to me, and that was why the envelope was so thick.

Finally I mustered the courage to open the envelope. I read the first lines of the letter: "Congratulations! You have been selected for the summer internship program." I could hardly believe my eyes. I had to read the letter several more times to be sure I'd read it correctly. I was ecstatic. Within months, I'd be on my way to Wisconsin to begin my internship. I cried from sheer happiness, thinking how far I had come in the last few years.

Once I'd gotten over the initial shock, I started looking through some of the information in the packet, which detailed my options for living arrangements and described some aspects of the program. I had several forms to fill out. One of the forms asked me to rank my first, second, and third choices for placement. I selected pediatrics as my first choice, pediatric/neonatal intensive care second, and medical oncology third. The letter said that I'd receive more information in the near future.

School and other aspects of my life continued to go well. I had been liberated. For the first time in years, I was really living.

In early April, I received another communication from the hospital where I would be interning, including a handwritten letter from my future nurse mentor, welcoming me to the hospital and the summer internship program. I found out I'd been placed on the pediatrics unit. I was so excited. I could hardly wait for summer.

The rest of the school year passed quickly and summer arrived. When I got to Wisconsin, I chose the dormitory housing option for its low cost and convenience. I also figured I'd meet more people that way, and indeed I did meet several other interns with whom I became friends. For my first weekend away, I decided to go camping with some of the other interns from the program, people I hardly knew. We had a lot of fun. It was a summer full of new experiences.

The nursing internship proved to be an invaluable learning experience. About twenty interns had been selected for the program from among several hundred applicants. Although we were all assigned to different units, we were oriented to the hospital protocols and policies as a group. We interns were frequently brought together to share our thoughts about the program.

On the pediatrics unit, I worked with my assigned preceptor. As I gained proficiency, I was given increased responsibility. Toward the end of my internship, I was caring for a full load of patients with only minimal assistance from my mentor. Over the course of the summer, I learned a great deal. I was lucky to be placed on a very progressive pediatrics unit, with a diverse patient population and some of the latest advances in monitoring equipment.

My Senior Year

Having successfully completed the summer internship program, I returned to school for my senior year with a new feeling of confidence. My classes continued to go well, and I resumed my extracurricular activities. Early in my senior year, I was elected to serve as secretary for the Student Nurses Association and co-leader for the Nurses Christian Fellowship. Being chosen for these positions bolstered my self-confidence even further.

Of course my self-esteem had its ups and downs. One day I was sitting alone in the school cafeteria, eating lunch and studying. One of my old resident advisors from the time when I was severely anorexic sat down two tables away. I hadn't seen Andrea in several years because she'd graduated. She was eating lunch with several friends. She looked over, recognized me, and started to talk about me to her friends, saying, "See that girl over there? She was in my dorm . . . She does look better, though. She's gained a lot of weight." I couldn't help overhearing the conversation.

Many of my closest friends had no knowledge of my past. It was my own business, and I didn't choose to share it with just anybody. Andrea's friends turned around to gawk at me. For the first time in quite a while, I felt like a freak again. Shame started to well up inside of me. I thought of removing myself from the cafeteria and going elsewhere to study and finish my meal. But I wasn't going to give in and leave. Hard though it was for me to remain in the cafeteria, I stayed out of sheer principle, vowing never again to hang my head in shame.

In my senior year, I faced a new set of challenges. The nursing curriculum required that I complete a rotation in public health; a leadership rotation in which we examined nursing management; and a rotation in mental health. Once again I would have to enter a locked psychiatric ward, this time as a professional. When the doors slammed and locked behind me, how would I feel? Would my old insecurities be stirred up?

I attended the first day of clinical rotations with my friend Tammy. When the doors closed, I started to feel anxious, and panic overcame me. *Oh no,* I thought, *I've got to get out of here. I don't know if I can go through with this.* Then reason set in, and I told myself, *You're just fine, and this is only temporary. Things are different this time. You can leave at any time.* I took some deep breaths and headed to the report room. Somehow I made it successfully through that rotation.

I'm sorry to say that the mental-health rotation was my least favorite clinical rotation. It wasn't the patient population that disturbed me, but the bad attitude among staff members. I was assigned to a clinical site at Memorial Hospital, the same hospital where I had been hospitalized at sixteen and held prisoner in my room for failure to gain weight. Our small clinical group was divided by pairs among several units. I chose to be placed on a locked adult psychiatric floor with one of my friends from class.

We were sitting in report one morning listening to a summary of the patients, their presenting complaints, and their progress or lack of same. While we were hearing details of a young woman's suicide attempt, one of the nurses said, "Ask me if I care!" Then she glanced down at her watch and said, "Oh, I guess I have to care until three o'clock." I was floored by her statement, and kicked my friend under the table.

The staff nurse's statement reflected her level of commitment to her patients and their recovery. It also reflected the prevailing sentiment of many of the professionals on the unit. I was appalled by this uncaring attitude and vowed that I would never work in such an environment.

Luckily, I had a compassionate clinical instructor of psychiatric nursing. She had previously worked as a nurse coordinator for all the psychiatric units at a major teaching hospital—the same hospital where they had made me walk around wearing a nightgown and a naso-gastric tube, the place from which I successfully ran away, never to return. Professor Pazzoli repeatedly commented on my "incredible insight." *How do you think I got the insight?* I thought. I rarely shared anything about my past, except with very close friends. Eventually I decided to share my story with my instructor because I trusted her. I knew she'd keep my confidentiality, and I thought she might learn something from what I had to say.

Kudos and Lucky Breaks

In December of my senior year, I started thinking about employment after college. I must have filled out thirty application forms, then I crossed my fingers and waited for an offer. I knew that the job market still looked bleak for new nurses. Only a few acute-care hospital positions were available, and all the advertised jobs required a minimum of two years' experience. As new graduates, how were we supposed to gain the required experience?

My lucky break came in early April, when the nurse manager from the unit where I had interned called and offered me a job. She said, "I have a part-time job open. I was going to post the notice on Friday. If you want the job, it's yours." I could hardly believe my ears. I had landed a real job. I didn't care that it was part-time. I had a job in the type of setting that I most desired. I knew there'd be opportunities to increase my hours later. I could relax through the rest of the school year, knowing that, upon graduation, I had a job.

Around the same time that I received the job offer, I got a letter saying that my name and a brief biography would appear in the next edition of *Who's Who Among Students in American Universities and Colleges*. I would also receive a pin and a plaque. I had been selected for the award based on academic achievement and contributions to my school through active involvement in multiple student organizations. The news of the recognition made me feel proud.

Just before graduation, I was inducted into the international honor society of nursing, Sigma Theta Tau. My friend Heather and I went to the campus mailboxes together on the day we knew the notices would be delivered. Heather said she wasn't going to open her mailbox because she didn't want to be disappointed. I peered into mine and saw a large envelope. "Heather," I said, "there's a big envelope in my box." At that point Heather could no longer stand the suspense. She looked into her own mailbox and said, "There's a big envelope in *my* box!" We opened our envelopes simultaneously. The letters read: "Congratulations, you have been elected to the Chi-at-large chapter of Sigma Theta Tau, the International Honor Society of Nursing." We started jumping up and down and hugging each other. I was so happy. All my dearest hopes and dreams were becoming a reality.

A month before graduation, I received a notice from the dean's office inviting me to pick up my honors cord for the graduation ceremony. The letter said that I'd be listed on the program as graduating Summa Cum Laude. This was not a surprise for me, but I was excited nonetheless. I had missed my high school graduation, but I was going to graduate from college in style.

Several of my friends went with me to pick up my honors cord. As we were walking away from the administration building, we ran into Andrea, my former resident advisor. I was hoping she wouldn't notice me. Once again I felt the old shame begin to well up inside me. I was praying that she wouldn't say something to embarrass me in front of my friends. At first Andrea didn't see me. Then she asked one of my friends for directions, at which point we made eye contact. I was holding my honors cord. With my heart pounding in my chest, I felt my shame gradually turn to pride. My honors cord was speaking for me. Its silent message was this: "I'm not merely surviving, I'm thriving."

Baring All

Before the graduation ceremony, my nursing class met for the last time. We were told that this would be a time for reflection and sharing. Everyone was supposed to get up in front of the class and share a memory or a word of wisdom. I thought hard about what I would say when it was my turn to speak.

One of our professors got up and shared a memory about her first experience in the auditorium where all our classes were held. As a very young child, she had accompanied her mother to class in the same auditorium. One of our two male students ran out of the auditorium and returned dressed as a woman, telling the class that we had brought out the feminine side of him. The class laughed uproariously. Other students evoked laughter by sharing embarrassing moments from early clinical experiences. One of our classmates said she wouldn't be graduating with us because she had failed the last clinical rotation. Her fellow students gave her warm hugs, support, and encouragement.

I contemplated trying to tell a funny story, but I couldn't think of any that would be appropriate to share. Then I decided to go for it. One of our professors was asking, "Who wants to go next?" No one volunteered. I raised my hand and walked to the front of the auditorium, getting cheers from friends as I went. "Go for it, Judy!" they said. I had never liked public speaking, but the encouragement from my friends was reassuring.

I took the microphone and said, "I remember my first time in this auditorium. Several years ago, I performed an orchestra concert here. I was the concertmaster, at the time, and I was planning to make a big impressive entrance. It was also my first time in high heels. The wooden floor had just been newly waxed and was quite slippery. I entered and almost flew right off the stage. So much for an impressive entrance." I got a few laughs.

Then I turned serious. "I know that a lot of you probably look at me and think that I have it easy." Most people knew that I maintained the very highest grades with relatively little effort. "Life hasn't always been so easy for me," I told the group.

"I'm twenty-seven years old. Most of you don't know that I spent ten years of my life tucked away in hospitals, struggling with anorexia nervosa. I never attended my high school graduation ceremony. I was kicked off this college campus on at least four different occasions. The administration told me they didn't want to be responsible if I died on campus."

"Many of my doctors told me I would never go anywhere except to a state mental hospital. Well, I've proven a lot of people wrong. Just remember that you have the ability to achieve anything you set your mind to. Don't let anybody tell you otherwise."

I received a standing ovation and numerous hugs, and there were also many tears. Now I knew that I was truly healed of anorexia. I no longer had to hide and feel ashamed of my past. I was completely free.

Graduation

On a warm, sunny day in May, I graduated from college in a beautiful ceremony, preceded by an inspirational Mass. Inside the splendid old chapel, the priest urged us to take our newly acquired knowledge and skills out into the larger world, and to use our wisdom to impact the greater society. I found his message very meaningful. Sitting on a pew next to Heather, I dabbed tears from my eyes.

The choral music was heavenly, and a warm glow suffused my body. It was a highly spiritual moment for me. A thought came to me: *I know how I can impact the greater society. I'll write a book.*

From the chapel, we were ushered down the weathered stone steps to join the procession. Soon my cap was flying in the air. I walked away from the ceremony with a baccalaureate degree in nursing and a new outlook on life. The world was waiting for me, and I was finally ready to step out and experience it.

12

My Life Today

In the months that will elapse between my completion of this book and its publication, I anticipate that I will have nearly finished the Master's Degree Program in Psychiatric Mental-Health Nursing at the University of Michigan. Upon completing the program, I'll be eligible for certification as a clinical nurse specialist. My goal is to work with people afflicted by eating disorders and assist them in achieving recovery. Eventually, I'd like to apply the profits made from the sale of this book toward the founding of my own treatment center.

What I'm Currently Up To

At present, I'm attending graduate school full-time, working part-time as a research assistant, and, in my spare moments, editing this book. The research work is exciting. It's a longitudinal study funded by the National Institutes of Health to look at the cognitive aspects of eating disorders. It's my hope that, by learning more about the thought processes that contribute to the development of eating disorders, we'll learn how to better prevent and treat such disorders.

During my spare time, I enjoy reading, writing, ice-skating, playing the violin, going to movies and concerts, surfing on the

Internet, spending time with friends, and drinking a nice cup of java with my sister. I try to maintain a sense of balance in my life, because I believe it to be essential for health, happiness, and over-all well-being.

Reflections on My Recovery

Many people have asked me, "What was the one thing that made you well?" I always stumble a bit while trying to formulate a response. The question seems a perfectly natural one. If I'd had strep throat, I could respond, "Penicillin." But the answer is not so simple when one is talking about an eating disorder. Contrary to what some may imagine, I didn't wake up one morning cured. It was a gradual process filled with many peaks and valleys, and it occurred over an extended period of time.

Probably the most important turning point in my recovery was my decision to become an active participant in the process. From then on, I was no longer a passive bystander; I was working to get well and to improve my life. Of course, I still had bad days. In time, the good days outnumbered the bad. Through many years of failed treatment, I learned that, in order to get well, I had to want recovery. Nobody could climb inside my head and make that change for me.

During brief moments of insight, I began to see that the one thing I considered my best friend and security blanket was actually ruining my life. In the course of my lengthy affliction with anorexia, I had alienated family and friends, spent many years in mental hospitals, put my college education on hold, and given up all of my hopes and dreams. I started thinking, *Maybe there's a bet-ter way.* If I was really honest with myself, I had to admit that I was miserable.

While sitting inside a locked psychiatric unit, with the possibil-ity of commitment to a state mental hospital looming near, I found myself staring out a large window. As I watched the people on the street below, I wondered, *Where am I going to be in five years?* I sat there for a long time pondering the question. Clearly, my then-current state didn't match up with the goals of my youth.

A short while later, I received word that my younger sister Anne was graduating from college. The thoughts inside my head began to race. Everyone in my family expected me to go to college. I was older than Anne, therefore I should have graduated first. Competitive feelings began to mount within me. *I need to get out of this hospital to go to college,* I thought. This renewed motivation was an important first step in redirecting into more fruitful areas some of the negative energy that kept me a captive of anorexia.

Anorexia nervosa became a central part of my identity and my way of living. In order to free myself from it, I needed to differentiate myself from the anorexic illness. My therapist, Susan, asked me to answer the question, "Who am I?" Her instructions were clear: "On a sheet of paper, describe yourself to me. If you were not allowed to say anything about food, weight, body shape, or appearance, what would you say?" Susan pointed out that I was much more than my illness. We simply needed to find out the answer to that basic question: "Who am I?"

Separating myself from the anorexia allowed me to view the illness in context. This allowed me to work against it, with my therapist as an ally. For example, I often came into my sessions complaining, "I'm so fat. I need to lose weight. I can't stand it." Susan would reply, "Okay, we both know that what we're hearing is the anorexia speaking. What do you know from a rational perspective?" I would answer, "I'm not fat. I just feel like it sometimes. I can stand it, and the feelings will pass."

The difference between this approach and earlier ones is that it allowed me to be a neutral observer. I never went away from the sessions feeling attacked or blamed for my anorexia. I always knew that Susan and I were working together to beat the illness.

I had clung to the eating disorder because I was afraid to give up control over the one thing I knew I *could* control. Eventually I realized that the illness gave me only a false sense of control, an illusion. It was scary to give up the one coping mechanism I'd grown accustomed to, but it was also a relief. Whenever I was tempted to fall back into old patterns, I asked myself, *What have you got to lose?* I knew that I could always go back to my old ways. The challenge was to find a better way of living.

During my recovery process, I learned to challenge the eating-disordered belief system. I used to believe that thinness would make me happy, that being skinny would improve my social life and would make me special. Looking at the situation from my present objectivity, I realize that anorexia made me severely depressed, isolated me from others, caused others to see me as some kind of freak, and instilled a great deal of shame within me. The eating-disordered belief system is based on lies that keep an individual stuck in the illness cycle. To recover, I needed to challenge and refute those faulty beliefs.

In order to relinquish my illness, I had to find other things to take its place. I sought out activities that I might enjoy. I worked to find other areas where I could apply my energy in a constructive manner. After years of striving for happiness through self-deprivation, I learned that true happiness comes from within. As other areas of my life became more important than my eating disorder, the illness began to lose its grip and to dissipate.

Finally, as other areas of my life improved and the illness lost its hold over me, my weight stabilized and then gradually rose to a normal, healthy weight. I achieved the weight gain by eating three well-balanced meals each day. I was careful to include all of the food groups (dairy, meat, fruits and vegetables, whole grains, and fats). I adhered to this diet with the same kind of perseverance that I had initially used to lose weight.

I've always been one who enjoys a challenge. Clearly, the challenge of anorexia is in achieving recovery, not in remaining sick. Once I reframed my goal, I was able to make a full and complete recovery.

If I could do it, others can too.

*   *   *

It's a beautiful fall evening in Ann Arbor, Michigan. The leaves are just beginning to turn colors . . . yellow, orange, crimson, burgundy, and every shade in between. The sun is about to set, and the sky has a pink hue.

In my fourth-floor room that overlooks the courtyard and statue below, I stand at the open window. A light breeze rustles the leaves on the laurel tree outside.

Sometimes, at moments like this, I think back and it all seems like a very bad dream.

But I know that it wasn't.

Sister Did We

scatter like loose earth, our black half-Chinese
    hair gone to seed.
You in Minnesota, starving into the plains, the
    broken trees,
relinquishing pulp souls. I played. I played
happy, played dead, played pretty, ate
words for dinner. You were with me, did you
    know it?
Did you pause for no reason, breath stuck in your
    spiny chest?
I was in your hospital room.
Call it telepathy.
Call it sisterhood.
Call it fluorescent-light spying—
I don't care.

Did we claw the ground bent-finger-mad?
    Remember?
Remember the hotel room, you hunched over your
    plate,
not eating, your wooden finger fidget, I watched you,
I ate, begged you, cracked-open begged you, stiff-
    legged asked,
"What do you want from me?" and you,
    "Nothing."
Did you root? Did I carry you,
second skin, bone under my bone.

Sister, I thought you would die, the flaky soil, the
perfection of your closed mouth—not yelling,
not raging the streets.

Did we rise? Did we uproot our crowning beau-
ties,
clumped with dirt, tendril gentle.
Your skull fattening, arms growing flesh. Did we
pass
18, 19, 20. The sky not caring, the sun in its
place.
You breathing, sister of my basement hour, growing
bones to walk on.

Sister, I wrote poems of you dying, the vomit,
blue tubes in your nose,
violin rotting closet.

Do we peel dead bark and look under? You,
Wisconsin Woman,
alive, my sister, at last. Your ears curling open.
Count
our soul rings spiraling.
I show you knot-hole, word, gnarled, poem.

You press up against it.
Say.
Yes.

—Anne Catherine Sargent

Appendix 1
Advice on Eating Disorders

How can you tell if someone you love is developing an eating disorder? How can you know for yourself that something is not right? What are the signs? I always tell people: "If you think there's a problem, then there probably is one." If you're in doubt, I recommend that you seek out a professional opinion.

The Signs of Anorexia

There are early warning signs. The early signs of anorexia nervosa include a rapid and intentional loss of weight; the skipping of meals; the desire to eat only in private; increased moodiness and isolation from others; cold hands and feet; drying of the skin; thinning of the hair; yellowing of the palms; cessation of the menstrual periods; and restless sleep. As the disorder progresses, its signs include hyperacute hearing; sensitivity to bright colors and bright lights; dizziness upon standing (caused by low blood pressure); and eating in tiny amounts, with strange rituals such as pushing food around the plate and arranging it in patterns.

How do you know whether your loved one is simply dieting or beginning to enter into dangerous territory? Prudent dieters don't lose more than two to three pounds per week. A weight loss greater than that means that the body is breaking down valuable stores of protein and fluid. A good question to ask is whether a loss of weight is actually warranted. A safe target weight can be determined from life insurance weight tables, which are calculated according to frame size. An individual should stop dieting once the goal weight is achieved. If he or she is unable to stop the weight loss, something has gone awry.

While trying to lose weight, the dieter should eat three well-balanced meals a day. Eating fewer than three meals per day will lead to nutritional deficiencies and cravings. The key to sustained weight loss, or weight gain for that matter, is lifestyle modification. For the overweight individual, add more exercise and eat less. For the person who is underweight, cut back on exercise and eat more. Extreme weight loss is never normal and should always be investigated.

The Signs of Bulimia

Bulimia nervosa is more easily missed, because its victims are usually of normal weight. The warning signs include spending a lot of time in the bathroom; frequent excuses to use the bathroom after meals; the disappearance of large amounts of food; visibly swollen glands on the sides of the face, looking like mumps; and weakness or tremors resulting from body-salt imbalances.

A classic feature of bulimia is that its sufferers engage in frequent binge-eating episodes. During an eating binge, an individual consumes an unusually large amount of food in a relatively short period of time, and experiences subjective feelings of being out of control. It's not uncommon for a person with this disorder to consume huge amounts of food—such as a whole bag of cookies, a quart of ice cream, and a box of cereal—in a single episode. Following an eating binge, people with bulimia typically try to purge the body of the excessive food through self-induced vomiting, fasting, over-exercising, the use of laxatives or diuretics, or a combination of these methods.

Purgative behaviors such as self-induced vomiting or laxative and diuretic abuse may lead to serious water and salt imbalances in the body. Potassium, an electrolyte or body salt necessary for normal heart function, often becomes depleted. This predisposes a person to serious, even fatal, cardiac arrhythmias or abnormal heart rhythms. Serious electrolyte disturbances are often asymptomatic; however there are a few signs that you can watch for. Tremors; seizures; generalized weakness; dizziness or light-headedness; cramping of any part of the body; and numbness or tingling in the extremities should all be treated promptly in an emergency room. More subtle signs of bulimia include the erosion of enamel from the teeth and sores on the backs of the hands. Esophageal rupture is an occasional, but often fatal, consequence of bulimia.

Recent Treatment Changes

In the years that have passed since I was afflicted with an eating disorder, many changes have been made in the American healthcare system. With the recent emphasis on cost containment, systems based upon outpatient treatment have become the norm, and systems characterized by lengthy hospitalizations are now rare. Each type of system has its pros and cons.

The new outpatient system requires individuals to assume more responsibility for their own recovery. Sadly, this means that some people will succumb to the effects of chronic malnutrition or severe body-salt imbalances and end up falling through the cracks. In contrast, the old system achieved significant forced weight gains, but the gains met with great resistance and were often not maintained. The continuing changes in health care have spurred hospitals to come up with new treatment options, which may result in improved outcomes for individuals suffering from eating disorders.

Where to Find Help

Given the changing health-care system, one might ask, "Where can I find effective help or treatment?" The answer is that many resources are now available to help in the obtaining of information, support, and treatment.

In the early stages of illness from an eating disorder, families, friends, and individuals themselves usually want to learn more about the disorder. Educational resources on the topic abound. Information can be obtained through using an Internet search engine; talking with your school counselor, family physician, or occupational health nurse; or contacting one of the eating disorder organizations such as ANRED (Anorexia Nervosa and Related Eating Disorders, Inc.).

Also, many good books on the topic are available at bookstores and public libraries. Books are a wonderful source of information. Many self-help books have been written to help people overcome their eating disorders. Some of the books provide a step-by-step guide to help an individual mentally combat the internal anorexic or bulimic voice. Other books address the issues of body image, self-esteem, and depression. One must bear in mind that self-help books are not the same as medical intervention or psychotherapy. Any individual who is medically unstable or potentially suicidal needs prompt treatment at an appropriate facility. However, self-help books are inexpensive and may be useful in assisting someone who is motivated to change.

In the past several years, the resources available on the Internet for eating-disordered individuals have grown by leaps and bounds. The World Wide Web hosts a wide variety of sites, including chat links; newsgroups; online support groups; personal Web sites and stories; and links to treatment centers and eating-disorder organizations. In order to access these sites, use a search engine and type in the topic of your query. The names of many sites pertaining to the topic will appear. (For Web site addresses and further information, see the Resources section at the end of this book.)

The Treatment Process

After a diagnosis has been established, a treatment plan will be formulated. Ideally, the person with the eating disorder will be an active participant in this procedure, and the treatment plan will be tailored to his or her individual needs.

Many resources are available for the individual who is motivated toward recovery. The treatment options may vary from community to community, depending upon an individual's school or work status, insurance coverage, and other factors. However, every community has resources. You simply need to know where to find them.

The conventional approach to the treatment of eating disorders involves some kind of medical monitoring program combined with psychotherapy. The therapeutic process is helpful in resolving the underlying conflicts that fuel the eating-disordered behavior. Contrary to popular belief, an eating disorder is not really about extreme weight loss or gain. It's about how one feels about oneself. A good therapist will work with a person to enhance self-esteem, assertiveness, and feelings of self-worth. When these underlying needs are addressed, the recovery process is greatly enhanced.

Choosing a Therapist

How do you find a good therapist? I recommend making appointments with several therapists, then making an informed choice based on personal "fit" or comfort level. Your therapist could be a psychiatrist, a clinical psychologist, a clinical nurse specialist, or a social worker with a master's degree. More important than the degree is the level of compatibility with yourself or your loved one. The therapist must be someone with whom the client feels comfortable. Don't be afraid to shop for a therapist. Make appointments with several, and interview them to see which one seems the best match.

Let the anorexic individual decide for herself which therapist she wants to see. If she doesn't like any of the counselors she meets, try again until she finds someone she feels she can talk to. In order to be helped by the therapy, your loved one needs to become a participant in the proposed treatment plan. When she connects with someone with whom she feels a rapport, she and that counselor will be able to develop a therapeutic alliance.

Several treatment centers offer a national referral service to help you locate experienced therapists in your hometown. If you need a referral to a professional in your area, see the Resources section in the back of this book.

Low-Cost Options

For those who cannot afford conventional treatment, alternative options can be found. Many colleges and large universities offer health services, including counseling services, nutrition counseling, medical monitoring, and even short-term support groups. Usually these services are free to the student because the cost is covered in the student health-services fee.

Individuals without access to university health services may turn to their local community. Overeaters Anonymous is a free, self-help, community-based support group. The organization has local chapters in many communities. The name is a misnomer, because people with all types of food, weight, eating, and body-image concerns are encouraged to attend. OA is based on the Alcoholics Anonymous twelve-step program. Many people find camaraderie and support in these groups. If you are opposed to a food- or weight-focused group, many other accessible groups, such as Emotions Anonymous, serve the same purpose.

Most areas have clinics where reduced-rate services are provided for people without insurance who cannot pay. County hospitals may be able to provide services or referrals to appropriate resources in the community. Another wonderful resource, available in many communities, is First Call for Help. The phone number for First Call for Help may be found near the 911 and other emergency numbers in your phone book. This service offers a twenty-four-hour live operator who can assist you in finding the appropriate resources in your area.

Some communities have therapy groups for individuals with eating disorders, run by professional therapists. These groups meet weekly over a period of several weeks. Usually there is a fee for the service, but the fee is covered by most insurance companies. The best way to find out about this type of group is to call the local hospitals. Ask to speak with the psychiatry or psychology department, then ask if they know of any eating-disorder groups in the area.

Starting Your Own Group

The city where I currently live has a self-help support center for people struggling with eating disorders. The center was created by a group of women who have recovered from their disorders. It is run out of a home and offers free support from nonprofessional individuals who are in recovery. The services are not to be confused with those of a treatment center or professional counselor.

The center offers women with eating disorders a place to go for socialization and unconditional support. The goal of the women who banded together to form it is to help a person to feel welcome wherever she is in the recovery process.

Your community may have a similar center. If you're interested in an outreach of this kind and your area doesn't have such a group, you might consider starting your own group or support network. I encourage you to be creative.

Afflicted Teenagers

Teenagers often feel motivated to seek help for their illness, yet are reluctant to talk about their problems to adults. Eating disorders, by their very nature, have a way of isolating sufferers from the world around them. The pattern quickly develops into a negative spiral of isolation, depression, and low self-esteem, leading to increased isolation.

The key is to break the cycle early in the downhill process. I encourage young people to reach out to others, telling them, "It's important to find someone you can talk to." The person could be a trusted teacher, an athletic coach, a neighbor, a grandparent, an aunt or uncle, a school counselor, a clergy member, or a good friend. Supportive friends and family are a valuable asset in the recovery process. Sharing feelings and concerns will help the teenager with an eating disorder to feel reconnected with the world.

Antidepressants

Although there is no magic pill that will cure an eating disorder, antidepressant medication has proven to be a useful adjunct therapy for some people. One class of antidepressants, known as the SSRI's or selective serotonin reuptake inhibitors, have been helpful in decreasing obsessive-compulsive behavior in some anorexic individuals and binge-purge behavior in a significant number of bulimic women. The class of drugs known as the SSRI's includes Prozac, Zoloft, Paxil, and Luvox. These medications are relatively safe but they require the prescription of a physician or nurse practitioner.

St. John's Wort, a natural remedy sold at health food stores, has gained recent attention for its mood-enhancing effect. Although there have been no clinically controlled trials of this herbal product, many people swear by its use. The one point that needs to be stressed with the use of any medication or nutritional supplement is that possible side effects must be weighed against the perceived benefits. All medication should be taken as prescribed, or as directed on the label. Finally, some people do not respond to medication.

Alternative Therapies

For those opposed to traditional medicine, or those who've received little benefit from traditional medical services, alternative medicine is a broad field that is rapidly gaining popularity. Alternative medical practices once frowned upon by the traditional medical establishment are gaining increased acceptance for their efficacy in treating common medical disorders.

Nontraditional therapies that may be useful in the treatment of eating disorders include relaxation techniques such as guided imagery, progressive muscle relaxation, and biofeedback; therapeutic touch; acupuncture or acupressure; carefully prescribed and monitored dietary supplements; and many others. Many of these resources will be available in your community.

Relaxation Techniques

Many good books have been written about relaxation. It's a technique that you can teach yourself. I used relaxation techniques to help reduce the anxiety that accompanied my recovery process, and found the techniques helpful. Quiet music with nature sounds such as birds, rain, or running water may help facilitate relaxation. Audiotapes of this kind may be purchased at most music stores. The standard recommendation is to use the techniques twice a day for ten to twenty minutes at a time. The techniques take a while to learn, so initially the period of time may be longer.

The Importance of Good Nutrition

In treating anorexia, the restoration of healthy eating patterns and a normal body weight is essential. Starvation leads to depression and a host of medical problems, including anemia; constipation; osteoporosis; hypothermia; vitamin deficiencies; low blood pressure; amenorrhea and anovulation; and electrolyte or body-salt imbalances. Other physiological effects include diminished thyroid function; hypercarotenemia or high blood levels of vitamin A; hypercholesterolemia or high cholesterol levels; swollen salivary glands; and, sometimes, cardiac arrhythmia, bone marrow failure, and death.

Good nutrition and a healthy body weight will correct these problems. It will also provide clearer thought processes to help the patient in working through the underlying psychological conflicts.

* * *

Nutrition for Eating-Disordered Individuals

If you are anorexic, improved nutrition will give you more energy, reverse the slowing of your thought processes, and decrease your obsessive thoughts of food, calories, and weight. If you are bulimic, you will notice that, with improved nutrition, you have fewer odd food cravings and a diminished desire to binge. The hardest part of starting on a healthful weight-eating program is the beginning. Once you begin, it gets easier.

At one time, my worst fear in the world was that I would start gaining weight and not stop. In the beginning of my program of improved nutrition, it seemed as if my fear were well-founded. People who struggle with eating disorders usually retain fluid when starting a healthy eating regimen. The weight gain is often very rapid at first, but this initial rapid weight gain is a water weight gain. The period of water weight gain is then followed by a period of rapid weight loss, as the water that was retained is shed. After this period, the weight usually stabilizes or, on a high-calorie weight-gain diet, very gradually inches upward.

There are many ways to go about setting up a healthy diet. The system I used was similar to a diabetic diet and consisted of counting individual food portions. Initially, the system worked well; it helped to eliminate my fear of losing control.

Most diets derive their plan from the recommended daily allowances provided by the American Dietetics Association. In this system, you count the number of fruits and vegetables, whole grains, dairy foods, meats, and fats that you consume in a day to come to the desired caloric intake. It's a convenient system in that it allows for some flexibility, and is one that you can easily teach yourself. You'll find many books on diet at your local bookstore or library. Some people prefer to see a registered dietitian—a good option if your health insurance covers this service. A professional dietitian can help you to formulate a plan that meets your particular needs.

Most weight-gain regimens advocate starting an underweight individual at about 1200 calories per day. The calories are increased in progressive increments, to the point where an individual is gaining weight steadily, usually at a calorie level of 2800–3500 calories per day. Weight-maintenance requirements are often set at a level of 1800–2500 calories per day for women.

Some people find it helpful to log their daily intake in a journal or food diary. I found that keeping a written record of my food consumption encouraged me to obsess about calories and food. However, for many individuals the daily food journal provides an extra sense of control and security. If it works, use it. If it doesn't, then don't.

Sticking to my diet was hard at first. I often rigidly steered away from the same foods I had avoided when I was acutely ill—foods I considered unsafe. As other areas of my life blossomed, my motivation to change the rigidity around my eating grew stronger. I really wanted to be able to go out with friends for pizza and a movie. I found that my strange eating rituals were still isolating me in ways I didn't like. Gradually, I challenged myself to add "unsafe" foods to my diet. Each day, I added a new unsafe food. Soon I was eating just like anybody else. The resulting freedom has been a blessing.

Appropriate Exercise

In order to balance a program of healthy weight gain or maintenance, moderate and appropriate exercise is important. This must be adjusted according to an individual's physiological state. For a severely emaciated anorexic person, light stretching might be an appropriate level of activity, combined with range-of-motion exercises to prevent the joints from becoming stiff.

For someone who is physiologically stable, a program of moderate aerobic activity two or three times a week will help to give a sense of control over the weight-gain process. It will also enhance mood, replace lost muscle mass, and halt or slow the process of calcium loss leading to osteoporosis that occurs secondary to chronic malnutrition.

I usually recommend that exercise occur in a controlled setting. This will help curb the urge to overexercise. If a specific exercise behavior has been problematic in the past, consider substituting another exercise behavior to avoid the temptation of reverting to old patterns.

In my case, running was a downfall. Once I reached a stable weight in my recovery process, I substituted step aerobics in its place. I joined a local health club and registered for a class, allowing myself to go to the gym only for scheduled classes, three days a week. When the class was over, I showered and went home. The system worked well because I started to develop pride in my new healthy and fit appearance.

Exercise trainers are available at many health clubs. Sometimes they charge a small fee for their services, but often this fee is included in the cost of the membership. A trainer is someone who can help you set up an exercise program specifically tailored to your needs. The person will ask you your exercise preferences, test your strength, flexibility, and endurance, and design a program accordingly. I used this service and found it very helpful. The trainer added some Nautilus exercises and light weight training to my program, which helped me to build back the muscles that had become wasted by my illness.

While a health club membership is helpful, it isn't necessary in order for one to have a healthful and controlled exercise program. The creation of a controlled exercise environment can be as simple as asking a friend to go jogging with you. Make sure you let the person know your goals ahead of time. For example, you might say, "Don't let me go more than two miles." Another way to accomplish the same goal of control is to limit your exercise solely to participation in volleyball or basketball practice. An athletic coach may substitute for an athletic trainer, as long as he or she knows the goals you're trying to achieve and is knowledgeable in the area.

Finally, some medical clinics have a department called sports medicine. This specialty service has professionals who can meet with an individual once or twice to develop a medically sound exercise program. Essentially, their function is the same as that of an exercise trainer.

The Dilemma of the Bathroom Scale

People often ask me, "What should I do with my bathroom scale? I know I should get rid of it, but I just can't seem to do it." Giving away my bathroom scale was a challenge for me, but it also proved to be a saving grace. It allowed me to eliminate the last vestiges of a disorder that had held me hostage for many years. It gave me the freedom to focus on other things and move on with my life.

Before giving up my scale, I bargained with myself about it for years. Ultimately, I recognized that action was the only thing that would get me where I wanted to be. Lip service wouldn't do it. As the old saying goes, "You just need to do it." Based on my own experience, I encourage people to get rid of their scales as soon as possible.

Sometimes a gradual withdrawal period is helpful in alleviating the anxiety that goes along with the change. The person who's weighing herself eight times a day can consider first reducing her weigh-ins to one time a day, then once every other day, then once a week. People with eating disorders are often afraid to get permanently rid of their bathroom scale, for it has come to be a security item. In this situation, I recommend lending the scale to a neighbor or friend for safekeeping. The anxiety that goes along with this change is intense but short-lived. The freedom that it will provide you is lifelong.

Confronting the Anorexic

Family members, friends, and teachers of individuals who have anorexia sometimes write to me and ask, "What do you think about confronting my daughter/friend/student about her eating disorder? I know she has a problem, but I'm afraid to talk to her about it. I don't want to make things worse."

I always encourage family members and friends to talk to the individual about their concern in a respectful and supportive manner. Usually this means sitting down with the person one-on-one and saying, "You know, I've noticed that you've lost a lot of weight, and I'm concerned about you. Is there anything that I can do to help? If you just need to talk, I want you to know that I'll be here for you. I care about you."

When I was obviously ill with anorexia, others were always afraid to confront me. Their hesitancy to broach the topic only contributed to my sense of isolation. It isn't possible to make things worse by bringing the problem out into the open. The worst thing you can do is pretend that it doesn't exist and let the person fall through the cracks like my friend Mary, who died from her illness.

After the initial diagnosis, parents often find themselves in an awkward position. Not wanting to make things worse for their daughter (usually it's a daughter, although sometimes it's a son), they find themselves walking on eggshells in their own home. A feeling of tension continues to build in the house. Siblings may start to complain about the unbearable level of tension, and may become jealous of the daughter with the eating disorder because of the attention her illness is monopolizing.

Parents sometimes write to me and say, "I'm so afraid that I'm going to make things worse that we're all tiptoeing around. The whole family is going crazy. What should I do?" First, tiptoeing around will not make things better for the person with an eating disorder. If anything, it will make things worse. When I was ill, I could sense apprehension in the house probably better than anyone else. The silence within the family, created by our failure to talk about what was going on, left me feeling alone and filled with shame. When my parents didn't talk, I was left to imagine what they were thinking and feeling. I have a vivid imagination, so you can only guess what kinds of things I was thinking. I encourage families to talk openly. When this is difficult, family counseling can be beneficial.

My Advice to Friends and Family Members

If you're a family member or close friend of someone with an eating disorder, try not to focus on the low weight and eating behavior. Instead, encourage the individual to explore her independence through healthy means. Provide her with growing room. Most important, don't enter into a battle with her over eating and weight. This will only exacerbate the situation. If the weight becomes such a problem that you're unable to focus on anything else, your loved one may need hospitalization for medical stabilization and the restoration of a healthier body weight.

If a treatment approach doesn't seem to be working, it's probably not. Don't be afraid to try something new. Remember that health-care professionals may not appreciate people who shop around for health care, and may let you know this. Don't let the careless or irritable words of these people get you down. Some health-care providers may even blame you for your loved one's illness or lack of progress. I know that my mother was the frequent object of such blame. When the health professionals resort to blaming individuals, they're really just expressing frustration over an individual's lack of progress. Remember that your obligation is to the well-being of your loved one.

A Message for Health-care Professionals

Please try to see the anorexic individual for who she is as a person, apart from her symptoms. Look beneath her gaunt exterior to the qualities within, the ones that make her unique. Don't reduce the anorexic person to a clinical entity or a diagnosis. Don't stereotype her based on your previous experiences with anorexics. Anorexia is only a mask that hides the inner person. Work with the anorexic patient to bring out the qualities that are hers alone. Help her to discover herself, to become independent, to grow wings to fly.

Be gentle with the anorexic client. Encourage her. Support her. Give her positive feedback. Treat her as you would want to be treated, or would want your daughter to be treated. Don't enter into a power struggle with the eating-disordered person. Within your heart, don't be angry with her, and don't blame her for her illness. She'll pick up on these attitudes, even if you don't voice them. Anorexics are extremely perceptive.

If you find yourself starting to feel angry or blaming, ask yourself this question: "Would anyone intentionally make herself miserable and endanger her own life in this way?" Remember that people are always doing the best they know how to do at any given time. The anorexic client, too, is doing her best.

Try to avoid the commonly held belief that anorexic patients are sneaky and manipulative. Yes, it's true that anorexic clients often try to sabotage treatment efforts. But that doesn't mean they're sneaky. The anorexic individual is under the influence of her illness. When a client sabotages your efforts, she hasn't been adequately engaged in the treatment effort. Work to enlist her cooperation. Stop to take a look at your own attitude. A negative, distrustful, or hopeless attitude on your part will only foster further resistance on the part of the client.

Work to develop mutual goals with the anorexic. Try to view your relationship as a partnership. Let your client know that, while you're there to help her, you don't profess to have all the answers. Help her to search for her own answers. Work with her to develop an individualized treatment plan that's specifically tailored to her needs.

In all ways possible, make it your aim to help the anorexic assume control over her own life. When she's unable to see certain things for herself, point them out to her. Let her know that she has choices. Help her to discover positive ways to gain a sense of mastery in her life. The offering of choices gives power back to the individual.

*　　*　　*

A Word to Caregivers

Whether you're a family member or a professional caregiver, be gentle with yourself. Take time for yourself. Make sure you're getting enough rest. Nothing is worse than a burnt-out caregiver. You need to take care of yourself before you can worry about anyone else. You'll be much more helpful to your loved one or your patient if you're well taken care of yourself.

Parents and health-care providers have a natural desire to try to fix whatever is wrong. Unfortunately, though, one human being can't take away the suffering of another. This is a painful reality. It's devastating to watch someone you love or care for suffer before your eyes and to feel helpless to do anything about it. Find support for yourself. Find people you can talk to.

Parents and family members, sometimes the best you can do is step back and let your loved one find her own way.

For My Anorexic Readers

Know that there is good help available. You may have to go searching for it. You may not find it on your first attempt. But it's out there. Don't hesitate to shop around to find the right therapist or counselor. A therapist should be someone you feel you can really talk to. Someone you trust. Someone you feel is on your side. Someone who doesn't judge you. Someone who supports and encourages you.

Weight restoration is essential to your survival. Believe me, I know what I'm talking about. I know what it's like to be sleepless, to feel chilled to the bone, to have it hurt you to sit on a chair, to be plagued by continual obsessions, to be stared at by strangers, and to always be hungry. I also know what it's like to be locked up in psychiatric hospitals with tubes jammed down your nose, to be tied to a bed in four-point restraints, and to be so depressed that you want to die. I have truly been there. That is why I can tell you that weight restoration is the only way out.

There are no compromises. I always wanted to compromise with my weight, but it doesn't work that way. A healthier weight will make your body feel so much better, and it will improve the functioning of your mind. The psychological improvements won't happen so immediately, but they too will come.

It's very hard to give up your hard-won achievement, the very essence of your current identity, the one thing that makes you feel special. But I want to tell you that there are so many *real* qualities that make you special. The anorexia and the thinness are fake things. We both know they don't truly make you happy. Strive to discover the unique qualities within you that make you like no one else on Earth. Try to find activities and pursuits that bring you pleasure. Work to find positive ways to gain a sense of control over your life.

Find ways to direct your energy into more productive avenues. Just imagine how much you can accomplish if you channel the same energy you use for the eating disorder into other areas! Develop some meaningful goals and work toward them. Your possibilities are limitless.

Even when things appear hopeless, there is always hope. My own story is living proof. Don't ever give up hope, and don't ever stop believing in yourself. You have the power to achieve anything you set your mind to. A full recovery *is* within your reach.

Appendix II
"What I Have Learned"

A Message From Judy's Mother

Where do I begin? I want to share so much with you—the things I've learned that may help you to help your daughter, your wife, your sister, your friend, through her battle with anorexia.

How little I knew at the beginning, which seems like a lifetime ago. How much I learned, mostly the hard way, as Judy went through her battle with anorexia.

I was lucky not to lose her to the illness, or to the mistakes I made along the way. I was terribly afraid of losing her. It was a fear that I carried with me every day, throughout her long struggle.

Let me share with you what I learned through our ordeal, in the hope that it will make the road to recovery easier for you to navigate.

It gives me pause to remember how, even before Judy's eating disorder became full-blown, I sensed that something was wrong. I had seen her discomfort grow, had witnessed a change in her attitude toward food, and had noticed a change in her behavior around food, as well. I expressed my concern to her therapist, one she was seeing because of her increasingly severe and intractable asthma. Although I distinctly warned him that I was afraid she was heading toward an eating disorder, he reassured me that hers was just a normal, innocent teenage diet—nothing to worry about.

I thought, *Well, I must be wrong. He's the professional. He must be right. Therapists and doctors are the experts. They would certainly know better than I would.*

My later experiences completely disabused me of that notion. I learned that it was best to trust my own judgment and my own gut feelings. If I had not learned that lesson, I would have lost Judy. Thank goodness I learned it in time.

I would like to summarize for you what we went through, and what I learned.

At the beginning, I could hardly believe how rapidly the disease took hold, and how it changed my daughter's whole focus and scheme of preferences. It shocked me to find out later that Judy had stopped eating almost entirely before her first hospitalization, *and I didn't even know it.* The excuses I heard from her had all seemed reasonable enough: "I've eaten already." "I'll eat when I'm hungry." "I'll eat later when I have time." I believed what she told me.

When Judy was first hospitalized, I had no idea what to expect, but I remember that I didn't like the attitude of most of the nurses who cared for her. They seemed harsh and cold, and some even behaved nastily. There was no warmth, no empathy, no reassurance. The hospital felt like a jail. I got to come and go. I can only imagine how it felt to Judy.

Had I known what I know now, I'd have taken her out of that program and found another one whose philosophy I could have agreed with. But in those days it would have been unthinkable for me to challenge the doctors on her behalf, to ask for information about what they were doing or question their rationale. In those days it would have been unthinkable for me to consider taking her out of their program "AMA" (against medical advice). Removing a patient from the hospital AMA is considered a serious breach of medical protocol and is widely frowned upon by the medical establishment. If a patient has left a hospital AMA, some doctors will even refuse to treat that patient—even on an emergency basis.

One program was recommended to me by a teacher at Judy's

school and by the parent of a girl in the program. I ended up having Judy committed to that program so that she would stay there. To this day, I deeply regret that decision, because I didn't first evaluate in full the program's philosophy, how it was run, and how Judy felt about the treatment she was being given there. It was a terrible mistake on my part. The doctor who ran the program told me my daughter would die if a commitment proceeding wasn't instituted to force her to stay. But his program wasn't carried out in the way it was portrayed to me. I was misled.

The program made Judy much sicker than she had been before. When she first went there, she had been able to maintain her weight, although certainly at a less-than-healthy level. When she left the program, after having been tube-fed for nearly five months—mostly in four-point restraints because she was opposed to tube feedings—she was suicidal, and desperate to lose the weight she'd been forced to gain.

Judy and I have since talked about this hospitalization many times. I've told her how sorry I was to have made a decision that hurt her so much. She has told me that she forgives me, because she knows that I was doing what seemed best. Luckily, she didn't die as a result of that mistake, although more than once she came dangerously close.

Judy's battle with anorexia was long, hard, and desperate. I know what it's like to watch your child lose her mental and physical health before your very eyes and to feel powerless to help. It's a kind of torture that only a parent who has gone through it can understand. It is an agony that is beyond words.

You want so much to help, and yet you don't know how. You try one thing and then another, and none of them work. I remember begging Judy to eat, trying to force her to eat, trying to reason with her—all to no avail. I watched as her physical health ebbed and her grip on reality faded, as her life became increasingly imperiled.

I truly understand the myriad feelings that one who loves a person with an eating disorder will feel, ranging from frustration and anger to hopelessness and fear. I know what it's like to try, time and again, to find new resources, only to repeat the seemingly endless cycle of rapid weight loss and grave danger followed by an emergency hospitalization.

It's said that even normal, healthy individuals can't survive two weeks if they fast entirely, with nothing to eat and nothing to drink. Think of how briefly a severely underweight person can survive, doing the same thing. I can relate to the gut-wrenching fear that other families know or have known, afraid that their loved one won't survive, that they'll awaken the next morning to find their loved one dead in bed. I have slept on the floor of Judy's room so that I would know if she needed immediate help. On other nights, I have wakened and crept quietly into her room so I wouldn't wake her, to be sure that she was still okay, still breathing. I know what it's like to be afraid. I will never forget how it felt to be so afraid so much of the time, for such a long time.

My close friends have asked me how I did it—how I went through the terrible times with such unflagging devotion, patience, and love. "I doubt that I could have done it as you did," some have said. I could only reply that if it were your child, and you were convinced that they would not survive without your unfailing love and support, somehow you would have found a way to do what I did. It's not that it was easy. That it was not. I agonized a lot. I cried a lot. Occasionally I got frustrated or felt fed up. Mostly I worried and felt sick about the danger Judy was in.

I drove through dense fog, pouring rain, heavy snow, and icy conditions that made the roads nearly impassable, with most of the cars and trucks pulled over to the side of the road. But I can say with pride that I never missed a visit when Judy expected me. I knew that my visits were very important to her. There was no way that I would let her down. She needed to know that her well-being was crucially important to me and that she could count on me to be there by her side.

My instinct as a mother told me that Judy would not survive without my total emotional support. I also knew that she didn't want to be a burden to me. She suffered so much. She was often depressed and desperate. She made several serious suicide attempts. But I knew that, more than anything, I wanted her to survive and have a life.

My love for Judy gave me the strength to be there when she needed me—twenty-four hours a day, if necessary—to let her know that I loved her, to offer her the company, reassurance, and support that she needed, and to make it clear that I did not blame her for being sick. I had seen others blame her and ask her why she didn't just cut out this nonsense and get on with her life. Those who said that had no idea what she was going through.

I knew that it was not Judy's choice to live such a tortured existence—cold, starving, and unable to think clearly, emotionally withdrawn and plagued by depression and obsessive-compulsive thoughts and behaviors. There were times when I saw her refuse water, saying that it would make her fat, when I saw her pluck at her thin arms, saying, "Look at this, this is fat!" She said this when she could connect her thumb and third finger, put them around her wrist, and pass them all the way up to her shoulder with her fingers still touching.

I can remember Judy saying, "I need to lose more weight, just a few more pounds." Then there were the times when she acknowledged to me that she knew that, even if she weighed only one pound, it would be too much. When I think of those moments, although she is now well, tears still come to my eyes. At times like those, I couldn't help but realize that my daughter was beyond reason, that her attitude and behavior represented a life-threatening illness and not a willful choice.

I was told on at least three different occasions by different doctors that Judy was hopeless, that she was schizophrenic, that she really belonged in the state hospital and that I should accept the fact that she wouldn't get any better. The words hit me hard, and they were crushing. But somewhere inside I knew that, if I chose to believe the doctors, Judy would give up and die. I share these memories with you now so you will know what it was like for us, so you will know that *no matter what happens, you can't give up hope.*

Sometimes I had no concrete signs at all to believe in, to cling to—nothing to give me hope that things would get better. But in my heart I knew that I could help Judy best by forcing myself to believe—by sheer will alone, if necessary—that somehow, sometime, she could and would get better. Keeping my hope alive in the face of adversity was the hardest part, yet, as I told you before, I was determined not to let her down. I vowed to myself that, as long as there was breath in my body, I would find a way to be there when she needed me.

I've been through it all: seeing the doctors believe that she was gaining weight when it was clear that she wasn't eating anything at all from the trays presented to her (*Hello! Is anybody there?*); odd food behaviors (I'll bet there isn't anything you could tell me that would shock me). All the things I saw that shocked me then only made me realize how sick Judy really was. They made me realize that she was truly fighting for her life.

Based on what I would call a mother's instinct, I more than once saved Judy's life. I know what it's like to call an ambulance and, with the help of the police, force your loved one to go to the emergency room while she denies that anything is wrong. I know how it feels, once you're there, to have the doctors ask if she's taken something, and—if so—how much, and to have her refuse to answer them as precious minutes (the window when an antidote can be given) elapse. I know what it's like to be frantic, and desperate, and scared to death. Even more than Judy needed my willingness to take charge when I thought the situation required it, I think she needed to know that she had my unconditional love and support—no matter how long it took, no matter how hard it was. I've heard about tough love. I tried it once, and nearly lost Judy. I wouldn't make that mistake again.

Out of all that I've learned, I consider the following the most important points to share with you:

- Give unconditional love and support to your afflicted loved one.

- Remember that this is a dangerous, life-threatening illness, not a conscious choice.

- Don't blame her for being sick.

- Find a good doctor to monitor her condition, *one who insists on a reasonable minimum weight and one who will enforce that minimum weight*—in the hospital, if necessary.

- Find a good therapist who can help your loved one deal with the underlying issues and conflicts that led to this problem.

- Find a way to believe that she can and will get better.

- Be familiar with the danger signs of an imminent physical collapse.

- If you sense or observe that your loved one is in imminent danger, *take action*. Take her to the doctor or the local emergency room. Trust your instincts. Watch her coloring. Watch for signs of weakness, dizziness, dehydration, or an overdose (vomiting).

- Don't be afraid to take action, and don't worry about whether she'll like your decision. This is not a popularity contest. This is about saving her life.

- If she will not go to a hospital or stay in one, remember that a commitment proceeding is always a possibility for a person whose behavior poses a threat to her own life and well-being.

- Seek the support of a therapist for yourself and your family, to ensure that you're handling things in a way that isn't making the situation worse.

- Seek the support of friends and family. Share as much as you comfortably can. Anorexia is an illness. It is nothing to be ashamed of. Let others reach out to you. They can be a real source of help and support.

- Get plenty of sleep, eat a healthful diet, and try to exercise as much as you can to relieve stress. You need to be truly resilient now.

- Try to get in touch with your deeper inner values. They will give you the strength you need to get through this.

- Remember that your loved one is fighting for her life. She needs your help. Ask her what she needs, and how you can help.

- Do not allow her to endanger herself. *No excuse or rationalization should allow her to go below her minimum weight without consequences (a mandatory hospitalization).* Psychological progress and steps toward recovery can't take place unless she maintains at least a minimally healthy weight.

Love can make a difference. Try to give yours in a way that will.

Resources

Organizations for Eating Disorders

American Anorexia/Bulimia Association, Inc. (AABA)
293 Central Park West
New York, NY 10024
(212) 501-8351
http://www.social.com/health/nhic/data/hr0100/hr0123.html

Anorexia Nervosa and Related Eating Disorders, Inc. (ANRED)
P.O. Box 5102
Eugene, OR 97405
(541) 344-1144
http://www.anred.com

Center for the Study of Anorexia and Bulimia
1 West 91st Street
New York, NY 10024
(212) 595-3449
http://www.social.com/health/nhic/data/hr2100/hr2111.html

Eating Disorder Council of Long Island (EDCLI)
82-14 262nd Street
Floral Park, NY 11004

(718) 962-2778
http://www.edcli.org

Eating Disorders Awareness and Prevention (EDAP)
603 Stewart Street, Suite 803
Seattle, WA 98101
(206) 382-3587
http://members.aol.com/edapinc

Healing Connections
1461A First Avenue, Suite 303
New York, NY 10021
(212) 585-3450
http://www.something-fishy.com/HealingConnections
This organization raises money for individuals who would not otherwise be able to afford treatment for their eating disorder.

Center for Counseling and Health Resources, Inc.
Gregory L. Jantz, Ph.D.
P.O. Box 700
Los Angeles, CA 90066
(206) 771-5166

Columbia Presbyterian Hospital
and the New York State Psychiatric Institute
(affiliated with Columbia University)
New York, NY 10032-3784
(212) 543-5316 or (212) 543-5739
http://www.nyspi/cpmc.columbia.edu/nyspi/depts/psypharm/eat
ing~1/index.html

Eating Disorders Recovery Center
8260 Northcreek Drive
Cincinnati, OH 45236
(513) 793-2666

Institute of Living
400 Washington Street

Hartford, CT 06106
(800) 673-2411

Johns Hopkins Hospital
Eating and Weight Disorders Program
Meyer 101
600 N. Wolfe Street
Baltimore, MD 21287
http://ww2.med.jhu.edu/jhhpsychiatry/master1.htm#edx

Kelly Bemis-Vitousek, Ph.D.
The University of Hawaii at Manoa
Department of Psychology
Honolulu, HI 96822
(808) 949-7232

Laureate Psychiatric Clinic and Hospital
6655 South Yale Avenue
Tulsa, OK 74136
(800) 322-5173

Mayo Clinic
Department of Psychiatry
200 First Street Southwest
Rochester, MN 55905
(507) 284-2511

Menninger Clinic
P.O. Box 829
Topeka, Kansas 66601
(913) 350-5553 or (800) 351-9058

Montefiore Medical Center
Academy for Eating Disorders
111 East 210th Street
Bronx, NY 10467
(718) 920-6782 or (718) 920-2176

Monte Nido
27162 Sea Vista Drive
Malibu, CA 90265
(310) 457-9958
http://www.montenido.com

New England Medical Center/Tufts University School of Medicine
Eating Disorders Program
750 Washington Street
Boston, MA 02111
(617) 636-5770

Newton Wellesley Hospital
Eating Disorders Program
2014 Washington Street
Newton, MA 02111
(617) 636-5770

Rader Institute
Washington Medical Center
12099 Washington Blvd., Suite 204
Edmonds, WA 98020
(800) 841-1515 or (310) 390-9979

Remuda Ranch
111 South Country Club Way
Chandler, AZ 85226
(800) 445-1900 or (520) 684-3913
http://www.remuda-ranch.com

Renfrew
475 Spring Lane
Philadelphia, PA 19128
(215) 482-5353 or (800) 736-3739
http://www.renfrew.org

Renfrew
7700 Renfrew Lane
Coconut Creek, FL 33073
(800) 332-8415 or (954) 698-9222

Rogers Memorial Hospital
34700 Valley Road
Oconomowoc, WI 53066
(800) 767-4411
http://www.rogershospital.org

St. Mary's Hill Hospital
Eating Disorders Program
2350 North Lake Drive
Milwaukee, WI 53211
(414) 298-6700

St. Vincent Medical Center
Eating Disorder Treatment Program
3140 W. Central Avenue
Toledo, OH 43606

Swedish Medical Center
5300 Tallman Avenue NW
Seattle, WA 98107
(206) 781-6345

The New York Center for Eating Disorders
490 Third Street
Brooklyn, NY 11215
(718) 788-6986

UCLA Neuropsychiatric Institute
Eating Disorders Program
300 UCLA Medical Plaza
Los Angeles, CA 90095
(310) 206-7125 or (310) 825-9989

University of Cincinnati
Department of Psychiatry
Eating Disorders Center
(513) 636-4737

University of Iowa Hospitals
Eating and Weight Disorders Program
200 Hawkins Drive
Iowa City, IA 52242
(319) 356-1354

Western Psychiatric Institute and Clinic
University of Pittsburgh Medical Center
Eating Disorders Program
(412) 624-5420

International Centers

Australia

Prince Henry Hospital
Eating Disorders Unit
Anzac Parade, Little Bay
New South Wales 2036
Australia
Telephone: 61-2-9382 5341

Prince of Wales Hospital
Eating Disorders Clinic
High Street, Randwich 2031
Sydney, Australia

Royal Prince Alfred Hospital
Missenden Road
Camperdown, New South Wales
Australia NSW 2050
Telephone: (02) 9515 6111

Canada

Homewood Health Center, Inc.
150 Delhi Street
Guelph, Ontario N1E 6K9
Canada
(519) 852-8413

New Realities Eating Disorders Recovery Center
200 St. Clair Ave. W., Suite 200W
Toronto, Ontario M4V 1R1
Canada
(416) 921-9670

Sainte-Justine Hospital
3175 Chemin Cote Ste-Catherine
Montreal, Quebec H3T 1C5
Canada

St. Paul's Hospital
1081 Burrard
Vancouver, BC V6Z 1Y6
Canada
(604) 631-5004

Toronto Hospital
585 University Avenue
Toronto, Ontario M5G 2C4
Canada
(416) 340-4896

Viola Fodor
The Wellness Centre, Inc.
P.O. Box 364
Campbellville, Ontario L0P 1B0
Canada

United Kingdom

Atkinson Morley Hospital
Copse Hill, Wimbledon
London SW20 ONE
England
Telephone: 44 (0) 181-946-7711

Hospital for Sick Children
Great Ormond Street
London WC1N 3JH
England
Telephone: 44 (0) 171-405-9200

Institute of Psychiatry
De Crespigny Park, Denmark Hill
London SE5 8AF
England
Telephone: 44 (0) 171-703-5411

St. Andrew's Hospital
Billing Road
Northampton NN1 5DG
England
Telephone: 01604 29696

St. George's Hospital
Eating Disorders Clinic
Cranmer Terrace
London SW17 ORE
England

Warneford Hospital
Oxford OX3 7JX
England
Telephone: 01865 226 430

Royal Cornhill Hospital
Dr. John Eagles
Cornhill Road
Aberdeen AB9 2ZH
Scotland
Telephone: (01224) 663131

Internet Resources

Web Sites Related to Eating Disorders

Anorexia Nervosa: Judy's Story
http://www.angelfire.com/ms/anorexianervosa/index.html
http://www.albany.net/~jsargent

The Something Fishy Web Site on Eating Disorders
http://www.something-fishy.com/ed.htm

Mirror-Mirror by Colleen—Eating Disorder Web Site
http://www.mirror-mirror.org/eatdis.htm

Lucy Serpell's Eating Disorder Web Site
http://www.iop.bpmf.ac.uk/home/depts/psychiat/edu/eat.htm

Cheryl Wildes—Eating Disorder Web Site
http://users.neca.com/cwildes

The Eating Disorder Site (by Pamela)
http://www.geocities.com/HotSprings/5395/

Tammy's Eating Disorder Web Site
http://sgtec.com/enchanted/ed/

Catherine Sundnes—Eating Disorder Web Site
http://www.stud.unit.no/studorg/ikstrh/ed/

Hazel's Eating Disorder Web Site
http://members.aol.com/hazel16042/index.html

Body Image Betrayal and Related Issues
http://www.geocities.com/HotSprings/5704/

Online Recovery and Counseling Services
Eating Disorders Recovery Online
http://www.edrecovery.com

Concerned Counseling Services
http://www.concernedcounseling.com/eating disorders/eatingdisordersindex.html

Mailing Lists

An eating-disorder-related mailing list can be found at the following email address:

listserv@ftp2.biztech.net

To subscribe to this list, type the following into the subject heading on the email message: "subscribe eatdis-1." To remove your name from this list, go to the email address listed above and type: "unsubscribe eatdis-1" into the subject heading box.

Another eating disorder-related mailing list can be found at this email address:

majordomo@samurai.com

This site is for individuals with eating disorders, their families, and their friends. To subscribe to this list, type the following into the subject heading box: "subscribe ASED-list." To remove yourself from the mailing list, type "unsubscribe ASED-list" into the subject heading box.

Still another eating-disorder-related mailing list can be found at this email address:

hub@XC.org

This site is geared toward the spiritual aspect of recovery. To subscribe to this list, go to the email address and type: "subscribe bridge-feed" into the subject heading box. To remove yourself from the mailing list, go to the same email address and type: "unsubscribe bridge-feed."

Chat Links

Something-Fishy Eating Disorder Chats
http://www.something-fishy.com/chatenter.htm

WebChat
http://pages/wbs.net/webchat3.so?
Go to the WebChat link above. Once you arrive at the WebChat address, go to the Home & Living area and click on the Health, Well-Being & Support option, then click on the Eating Disorder Room.

Eating Disorders Chatroom
http://www.geocities.com/Wellesley/4220/chat.html

Talk City
http://www.talkcity.com
Go to the Talk City link above. Once you arrive at the site, look under "Communities" and click on "Transformations," which is a self-help and recovery site.

Newsgroups

Alt.support.eating-disord
This newsgroup is eating-disorders-related.

Alt.support.depression
This newsgroup is for individuals affected by depression (not a specific eating-disorders focus).

Alt.support.anxiety-panic
This newsgroup is for individuals affected by anxiety or panic (not a specific eating-disorders focus).

Alt.support.obesity
This newsgroup is geared toward individuals who are over-weight.

Alt.support.big-folks
Another newsgroup for overweight individuals. The emphasis is on body acceptance and healthful living.

Self-Help Books on Eating Disorders

For information

Bitter, Cynthia. *Good Enough: When Losing Is Winning, Perfection Becomes Obsession, and Thin Enough Can Never Be Achieved.* Penfield, NY: Hopelines, 1998

Bruch, Hilde. *Conversations with Anorexics: A Compassionate and Hopeful Journey through the Therapeutic Process.* Edited by Czyzewski D, Suhr M. New York: Basic Books, 1988.

————. *Eating Disorders: Obesity, Anorexia Nervosa, and the Person Within.* New York: Basic Books, 1973.

————. *The Golden Cage: The Enigma of Anorexia Nervosa.* Cambridge, MA: Harvard University Press, 1978.

Chernin, Kim. *The Hungry Self: Women, Eating, and Identity.* New York: Random House, 1985.

Costin, Carolyn. *The Eating Disorders Sourcebook: A Comprehensive Guide to the Causes, Treatments, and Prevention of Eating Disorders.* Los Angeles: Lowell House, 1996.

Garner, D., and P. Garfinkel. *Handbook of Treatment for Eating Disorders.* New York: Guilford Press, 1997.

Hall, Lindsey. *Full Lives: Women Who Have Freed Themselves From Food and Weight Obsession.* Carlsbad, CA: Gurze Books, 1993.

Hirschmann, J. R., and C. H. Munter. *Overcoming Overeating.* New York: Fawcett Books, 1989.

Hirschmann, J. R., and L. Zaphiropoulous. *Preventing Childhood Eating Problems: A Practical, Positive Approach to Raising Children Free of Food and Weight Conflicts.* Carlsbad, CA: Gurze Books, 1993.

Latimer, Jane. *Beyond the Food Game: A Spiritual and Psychological Approach to Healing Emotional Eating.* Denver, CO: Livingquest, 1993.

————. *Living Binge-Free: A Personal Guide to Victory Over Compulsive Eating.* Denver, CO: Livingquest, 1988.

Levenkron, Steven. *Treating and Overcoming Anorexia Nervosa.* New York: Warner Books, 1987.

Maine, Margo. *Father Hunger: Fathers, Daughters, and Food.* Carlsbad, CA: Gurze Books, 1991.

Palmer, R. L. *Anorexia Nervosa: A Guide for Sufferers and Their Families.* New York: Penguin USA, 1989.

Pipher, M. *Hunger Pains: The Modern Woman's Tragic Quest for Thinness.* New York: Ballantine Books, 1997.

————. *Reviving Ophelia: Saving the Selves of Adolescent Girls.* New York: Ballantine Books, 1994.

Rumney, Avis. *Dying to Please: Anorexia Nervosa and Its Cure.* Jefferson, NC: McFarland & Company, 1983.

Sacker, Ira, and Marc Zimmer. *Dying to Be Thin: Understanding and Defeating Anorexia Nervosa and Bulimia—A Practical, Life-saving Guide.* New York: Warner Books, 1987.

Siegel, M., J. Brisman, and M. Weinshel. *Surviving an Eating Disorder: Perspectives and Strategies for Family and Friends.* New York: HarperCollins, 1989.

Way, Karen. *Anorexia Nervosa and Recovery: A Hunger for Meaning.* Binghamton, NY: Haworth Press, 1993.

For support

Cohen, Mary Anne. *French Toast for Breakfast: Declaring Peace With Emotional Eating.* Carlsbad, CA: Gurze Books, 1995.

Crisp, Arthur. *Anorexia Nervosa: The Wish to Change.* New York: Taylor & Francis, 1996.

Fodor, Viola. *Desperately Seeking Self: A Guidebook for People with Eating Disorders.* Carlsbad, CA: Gurze Books, 1994.

Hall, L., and M. Ostroff. *Anorexia Nervosa: A Guide to Recovery.* Carlsbad, CA: Gurze Books, 1998.

Hall, L., and L. Cohn. *Bulimia: A Guide to Recovery.* Carlsbad, CA: Gurze Books, 1992.

Hirschmann, J., and C. Munter. *When Women Stop Hating Their Bodies: Freeing Yourself from Food and Weight Obsession.* New York: Fawcett Books, 1995.

Jantz, Gregory. *Hope, Help, and Healing for Eating Disorders: A New Approach to Treating Anorexia, Bulimia, and Overeating.* Wheaton, Illinois: Harold Shaw Publishers, 1995.

Johnston, Joni. *Appearance Obsession: Learning to Love the Way You Look.* Deerfield Beach, FL: Health Communications Inc., 1994.

Kano, Susan. *Making Peace with Food: Freeing Yourself from the Diet-Weight Obsession.* New York: Harper & Row, 1989.

Rodin, Judith. *Body Traps.* Harlingen, TX: Quill Books, 1993.

Sandbek, Terence. *The Deadly Diet: Recovering From Anorexia and Bulimia.* Oakland, CA: New Harbinger Publications, 1986.

Other self-help books

Burns, David. *Feeling Good: The New Mood Therapy.* New York: Avon Books, 1988.

————. *Feeling Good Handbook.* New York: Plume, 1989.

Copeland, Mary Ellen. *The Depression Workbook: A Guide for Living with Depression and Manic Depression.* Oakland, CA: New Harbinger Publications, 1992.

McKay, M., and P. Fanning. *Self-Esteem.* Oakland, CA: New Harbinger Publications, 1993.

Books on relaxation

Benson, Herbert. *The Relaxation Response.* New York: Avon Books, 1976.

————. *The Wellness Book: The Comprehensive Guide to Maintaining Health and Treating Stress-Related Illness.* New York: Fireside, 1993.

Davis, M., E. R. Eshelman, and M. McKay. *The Relaxation and Stress-Reduction Workbook.* Oakland, CA: New Harbinger Publications, 1995.

Naparstek, Belleruth. *Staying Well With Guided Imagery.* New York: Warner Books, 1995.

Books on nutrition

Duyff, R. L. *The American Dietetic Association's Complete Food and Nutrition Guide.* New York: Chronimed Publishers, 1996.

Finn, S., and J. Tougas. *The American Dietetic Association Guide to Women's Nutrition for Healthy Living.* New York: Perigee Publishers, 1997.

Somer, Elizabeth. *Food and Mood: The Complete Guide to Eating Well and Feeling Your Best.* New York: Henry Holt, 1996.

Index

Other outstanding relationship books

Dancing in the Dark
The Shadow Side of Intimate Relationships
Douglas & Naomi Moseley

"A + √ [TOP RATING]. This book is not for the faint-hearted, but it is for those who want to take their relationship to a glorious level—and are willing to do the work in the shadows to get there."
Marriage Magazine

"Bravo! Brava! Finally a book with real solutions for real relationships . . . a must-read for individuals, couples, and helping professionals."
Pat Love, Ed.D., co-author, *Hot Monogamy*

Fishing by Moonlight
The Art of Choosing Intimate Partners
Colene Sawyer, Ph.D.

Winner: 1997 Clark Vincent Award from the California Association of Marriage and Family Therapists

"From healing past pain to preparing for a healthy mate, this book is filled with useful insights."
John Gray, Ph.D., author, *Men Are From Mars, Women Are From Venus*

Riding the Dragon
The Power of Committed Relationship
Rhea Powers & Gawain Bantle

"A radically fresh, challenging, and inspired path into vastly expanded personal and mutual development attainable through a committed relationship."
W. Brugh Joy, M.D., author, *Joy's Way* and *Avalanche*

"A wise, bold, honest map through the maze of intimate relationship. Rhea and Gawain are delightful mirrors, reflecting hope, courage, and inspiration for all lovers."
Gabrielle Roth, author, *Maps to Ecstasy: Teachings of an Urban Shaman*

Other outstanding transition books

The Care and Feeding of Perfectionists
Cynthia Curnan, Ph.D.

"The Perfectionist is one of the major league hitters in the family of selves that live within each of us. In this book, Cynthia brings clarity as to how the Perfectionist operates, the mischief it can cause in our personality, and, most importantly, she shows us how to deal with our perfectionism in everyday life. This book will serve health care givers as well as the general public, and we strongly recommend it to you."
Hal Stone, Ph.D., and Sidra Stone Ph.D.
Authors, *Embracing Our Selves*
and *Embracing Your Inner Critic*

Strings: The Miracle of Life
John B. Robbins

"Robbins brilliantly details the incredible complex, miraculous, and intricate world of medicine . . . a roller coaster of suspense that the reader will find difficult to put down . . . will both inspire readers and deepen their spirituality. Highly recommended."
Foreword Magazine

". . . incredible page-turning account . . . Around this true medical thriller is woven a wonderfully articulate description of Robbin's own Buddhist perspectives, and the wrestling he does with the contradictions, paradoxes, and ironies of American medicine and of life itself."
NAPRA ReView

Spirituality
Where Body and Soul Encounter the Sacred
Carl McColman

"Spirituality provides multiple doorways of comfort and insight . . . a practical book for personal, professional, and deep interior exploration."
Angeles Arrien, Ph.D., Cultural Anthropologist, author,
The Four-Fold Way and *Signs of Life*

"Carl McColman writes from within a clear religious tradition, but in a way which is open and accessible to people who are struggling with what they con believe. His book will be of great help to many people."
Kenneth Leech, author, *Soul Friend* and *True Prayer*